Tom R. Farr

# Til Death We Do Art.
## An Adult Coloring Book

Copyright © 2018 Texas T Ventures LLC
First Edition

# Artist's Note

All right....this ought to keep you busy for a while. I added a (mostly) blank page beside the drawings so you can add your doodles, deep thoughts, poems, grocery lists and whatever comes to mind.

I suppose most adult coloring books have bright, colorful covers with an example of how you might color in the pages. I suspect that if you have made it past the cover and have seen a few of my drawings, you are probably not the sort of colorist who would take kindly to any ideas I might have about what hues you should use.

The drawings are in the same sequence as they were in my sketchbook. I had to cut it up to scan the pages, so it just seemed right to lay this book out like it tumbled out of my (ok, go ahead and say it...."very strange") mind.

I hope these pages bring you some moments of peace, joy and love. I know, some of the drawings are pretty bizarre, but maybe some of them will open a little window somewhere in your mind that will let a big idea slip out while you are letting your hand and eyes play and your mind rest. I had a lot of fun making the pictures.

T.R.F.

Copyright © 2018 Texas T Ventures LLC

This page intentionally blank: Your turn....Fill it up!

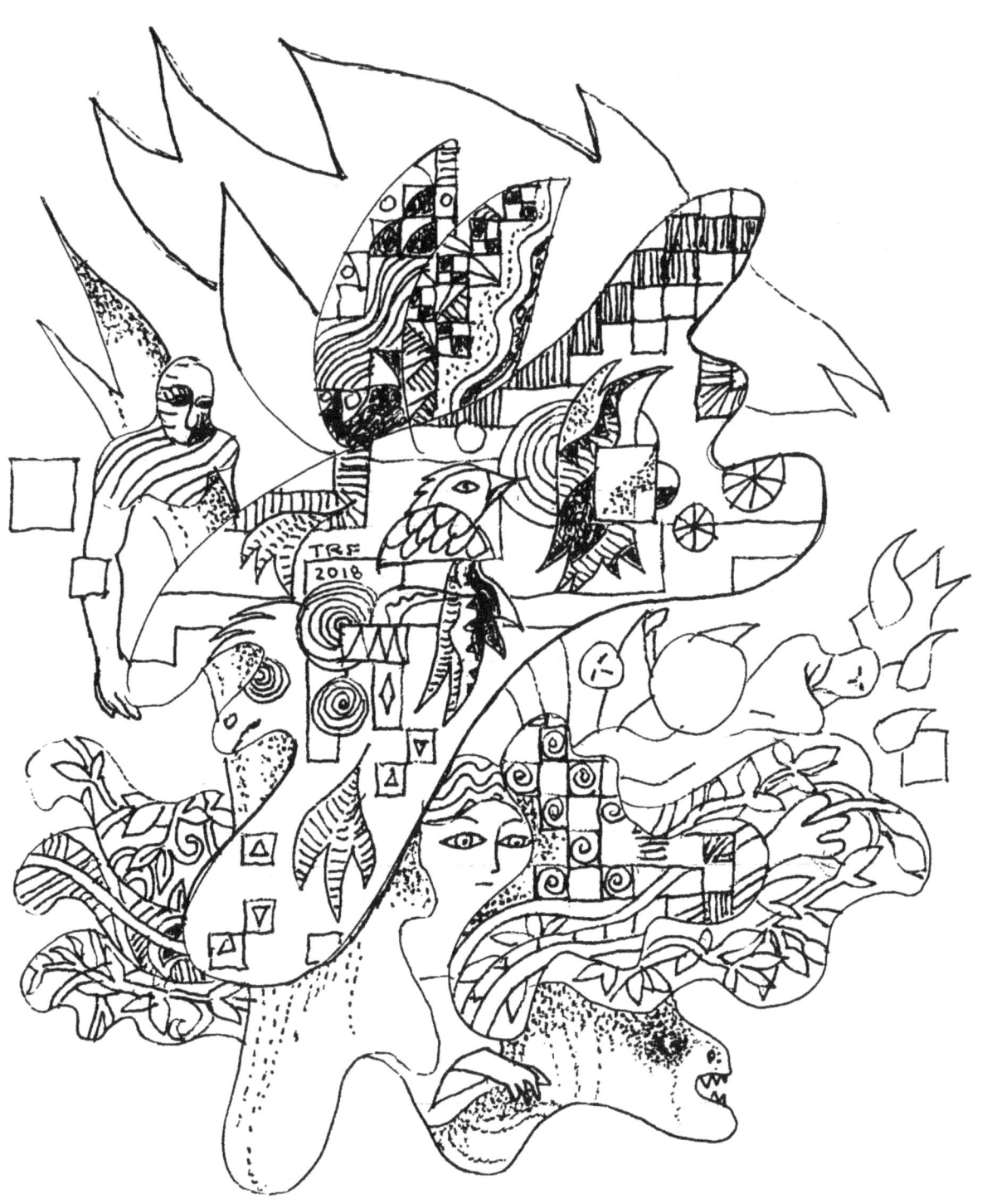

A few of the drawings have titles. I call this one "Death by Customer."

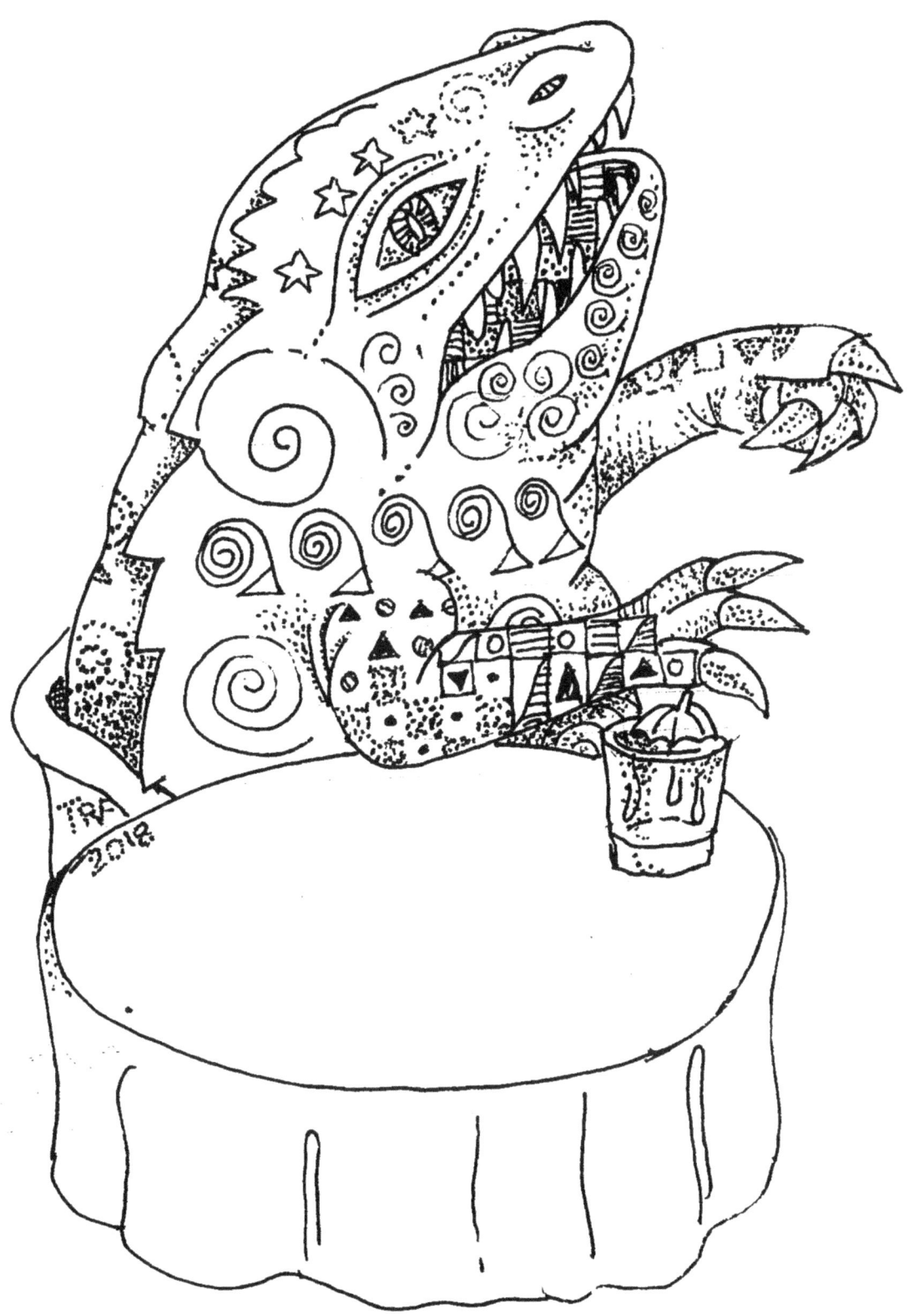

Are you filling these blank pages up? I'm not killing trees for no reason. (This drawing is titled "Soldier On!").

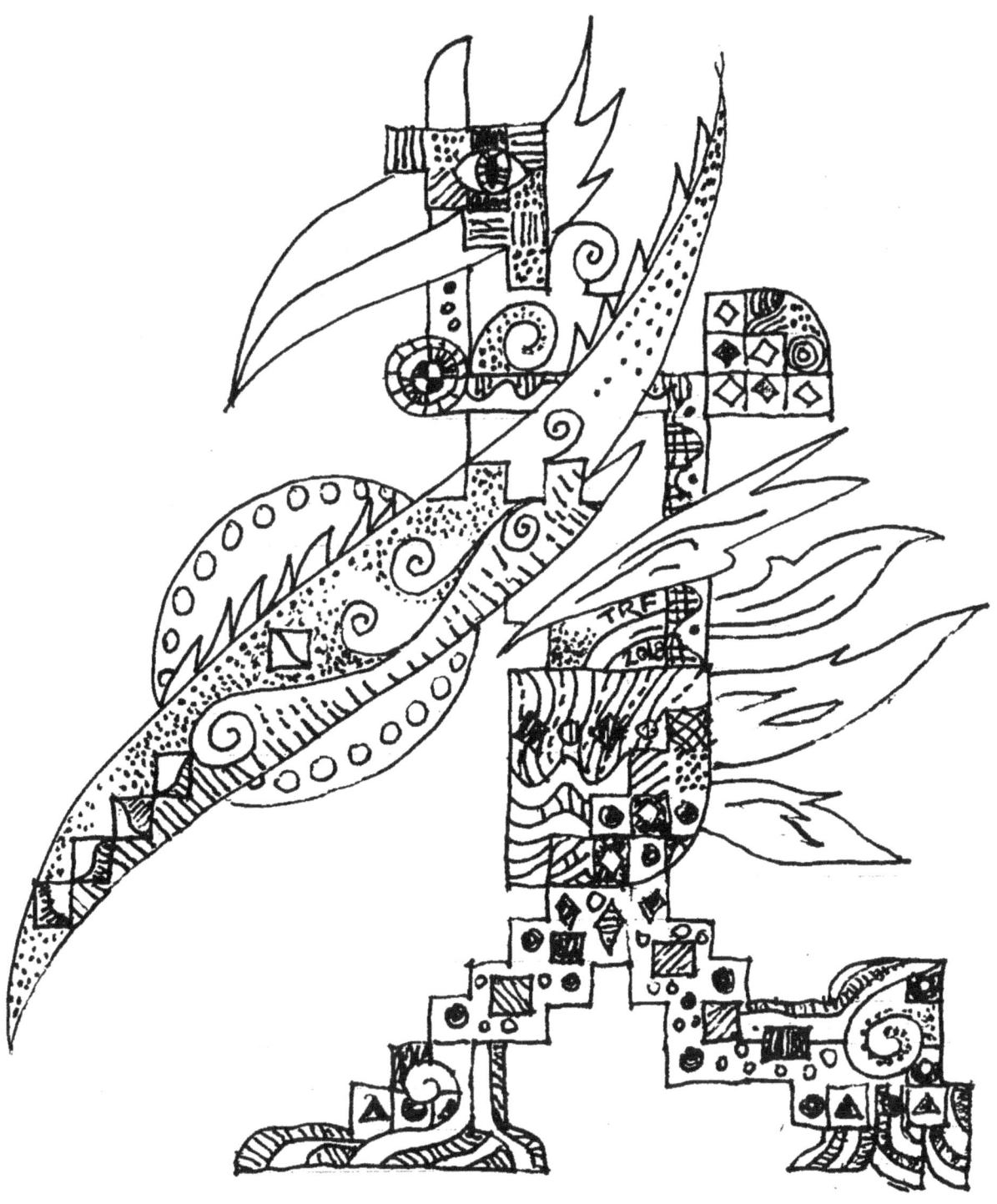

WOW! a grid for those who like to stay in the lines. I used a grid like this to get outside the lines with the drawings in this book. Don't worry, I won't put it on all of the blank pages.....but how about every other one?

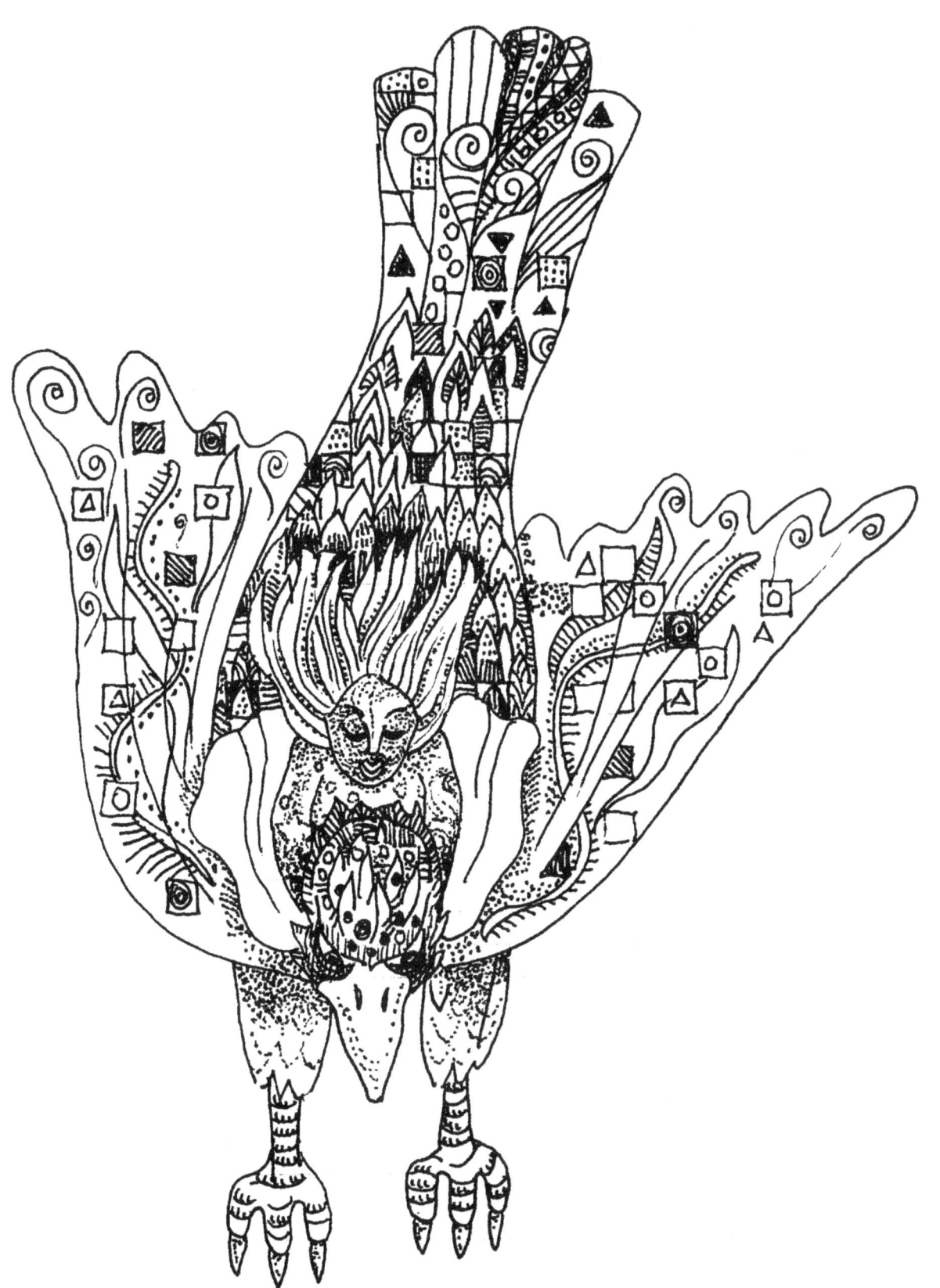

Do you ever dream you can fly?

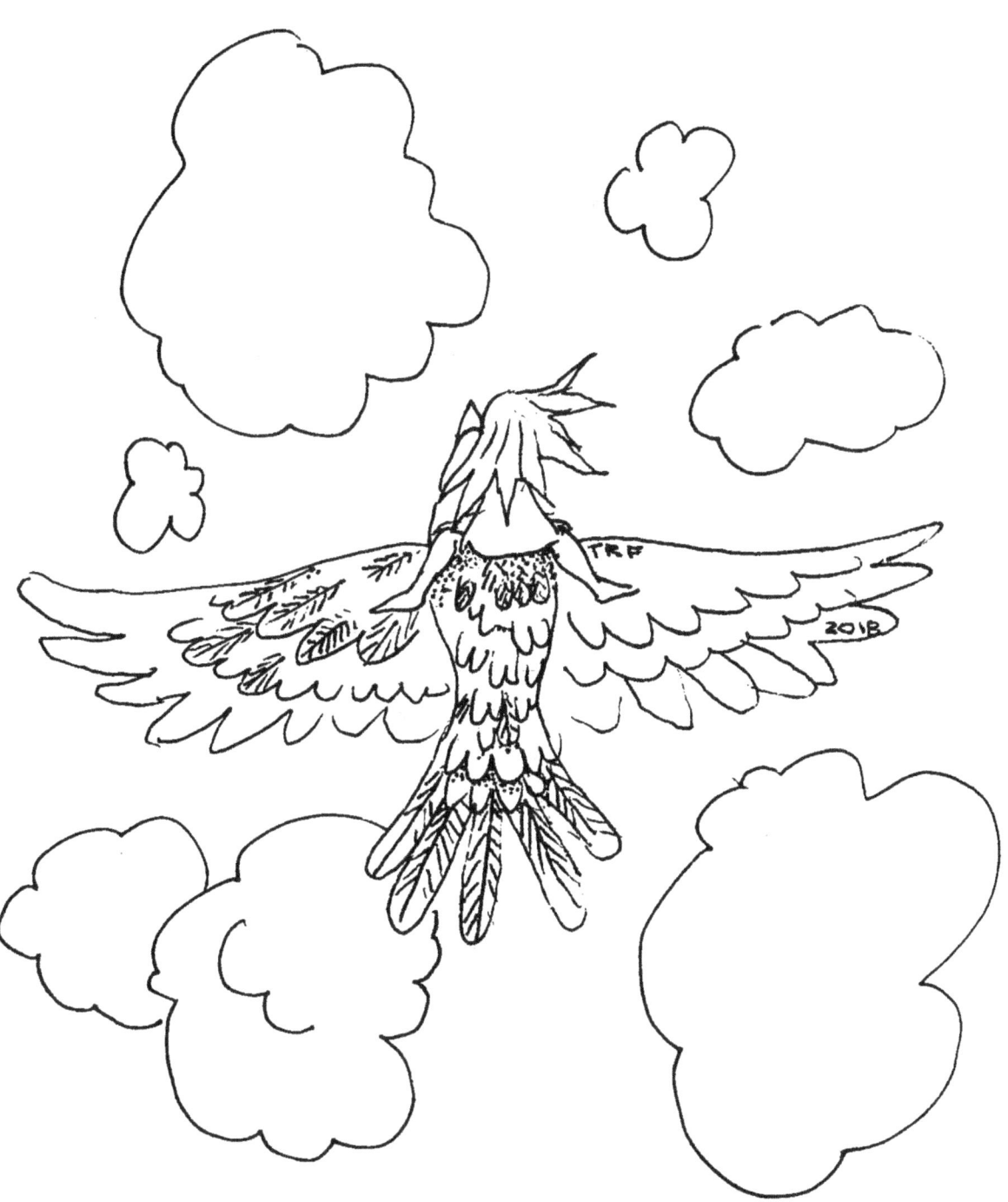

Do you work your way straight through a project from beginning to end? If so, this is your last chance to bail out before things get too weird.

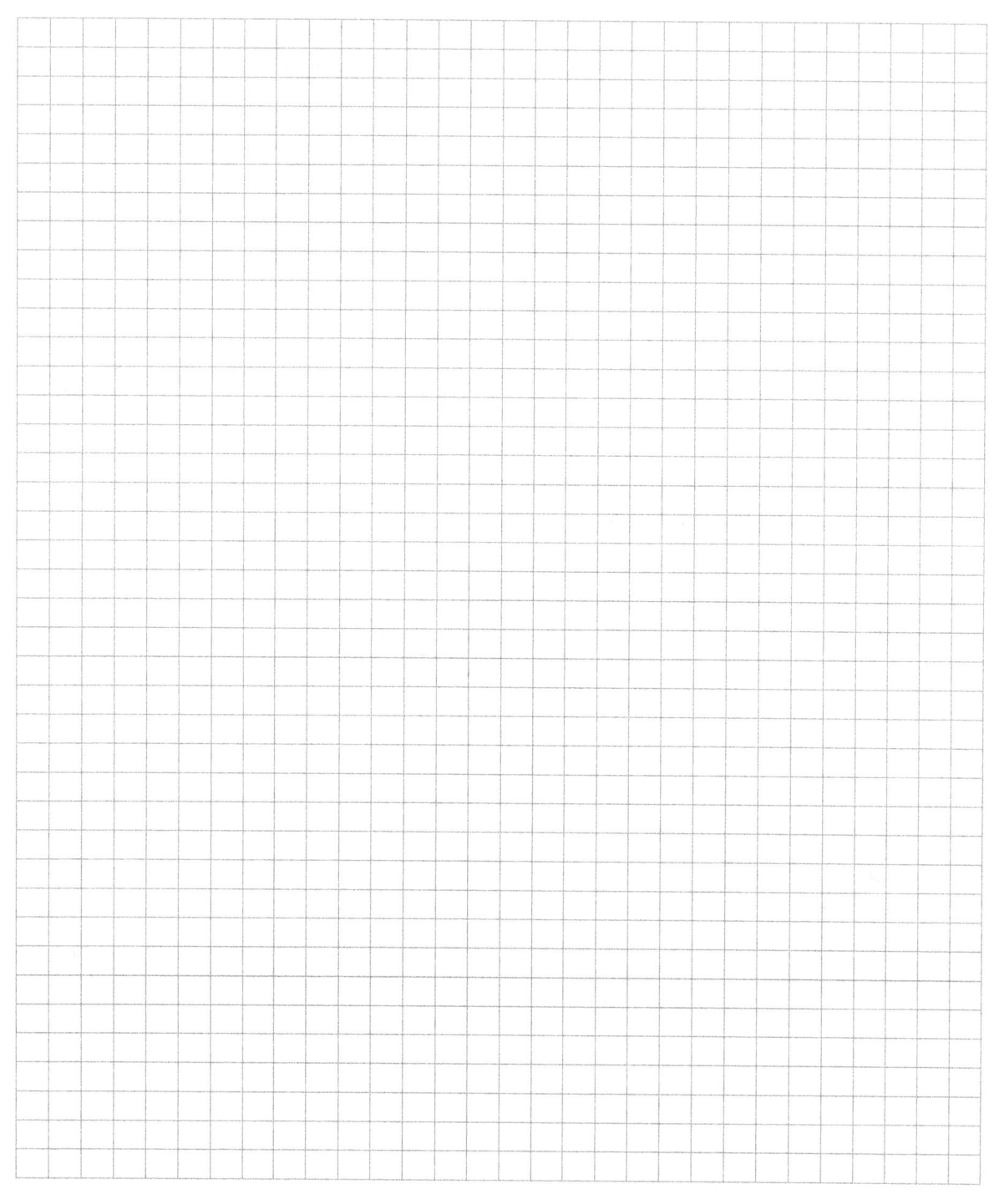

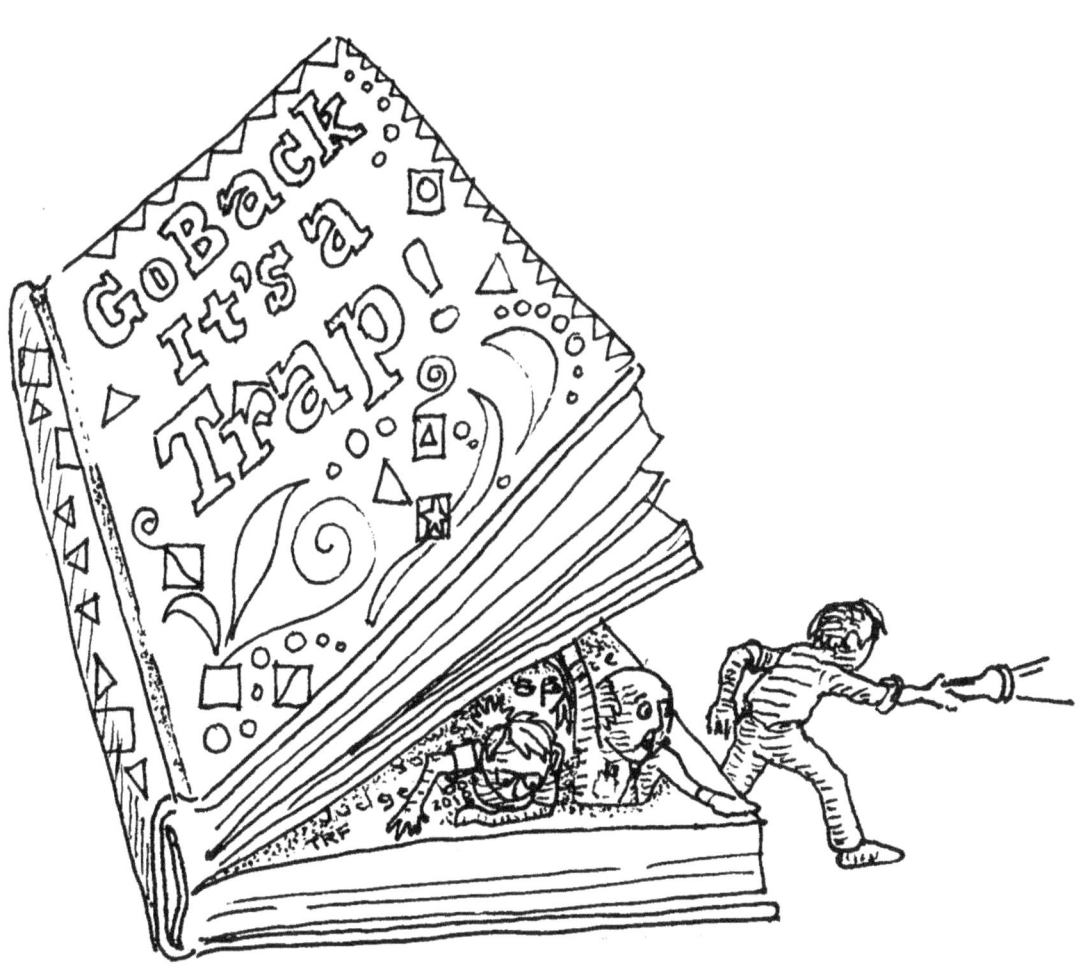

# What's on your mind?

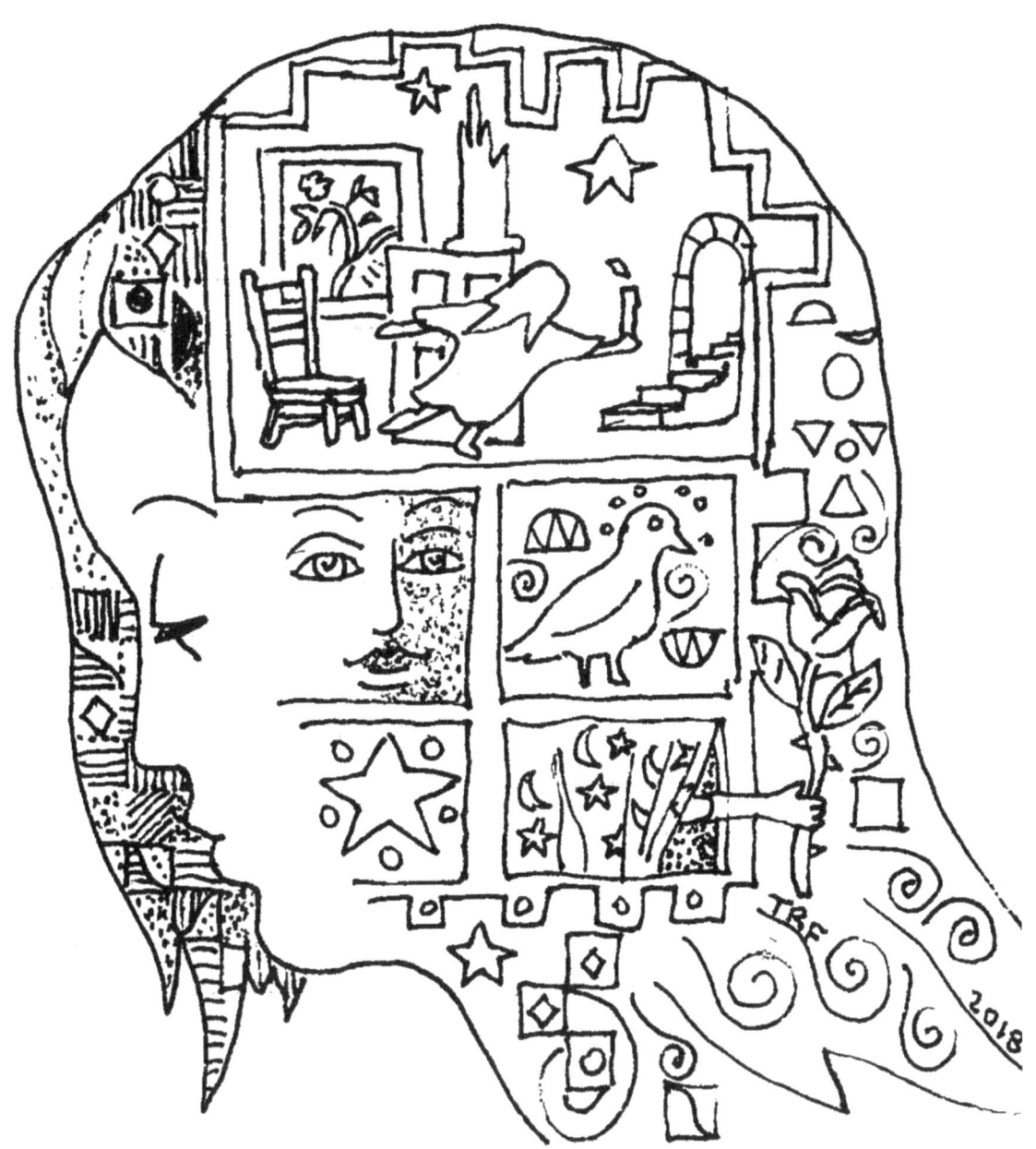

So many pages to color...
So little time.

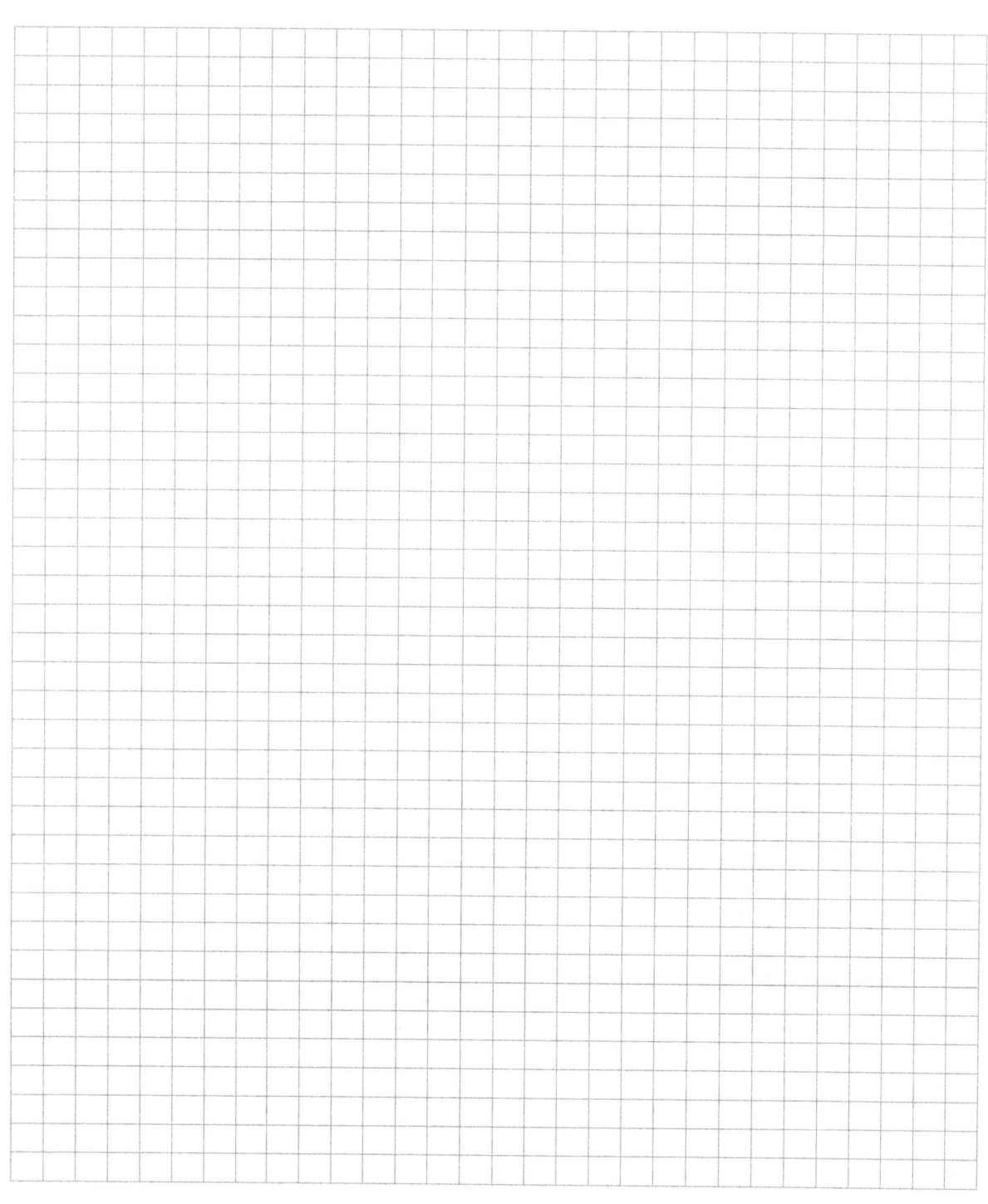

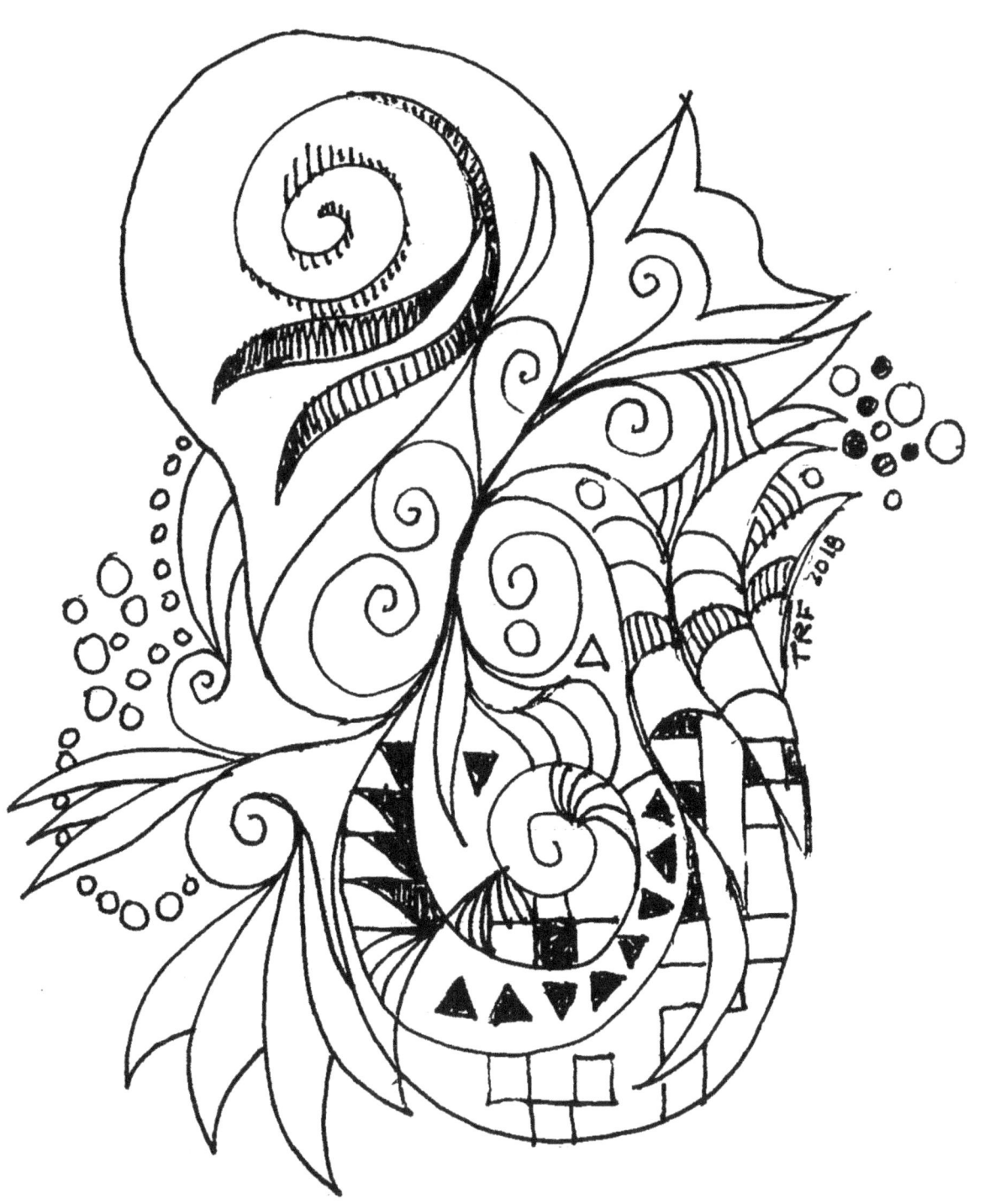

Shameless commerce warning:
This drawing is available on
one of my t-shirts

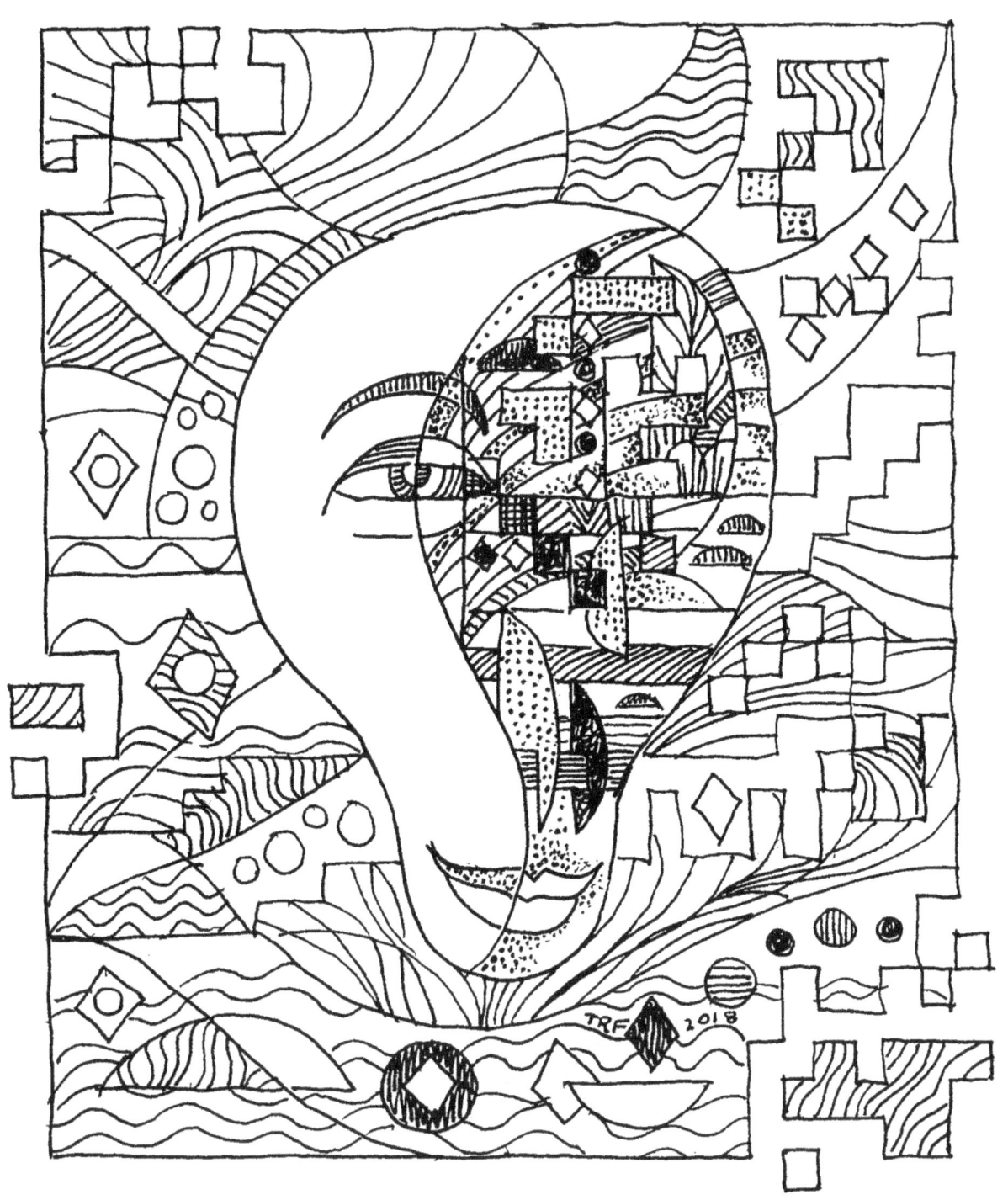

Deep thought goes here:

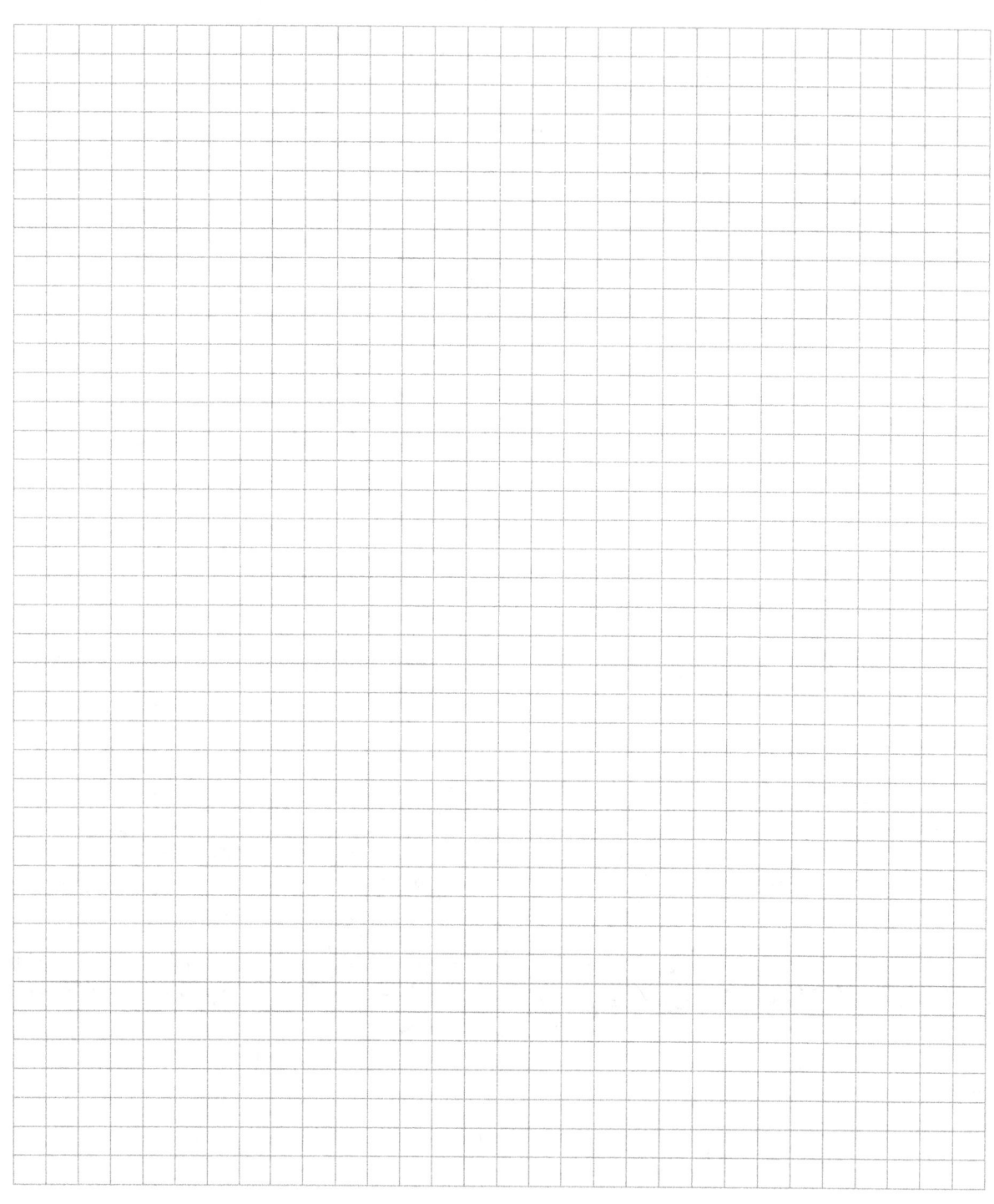

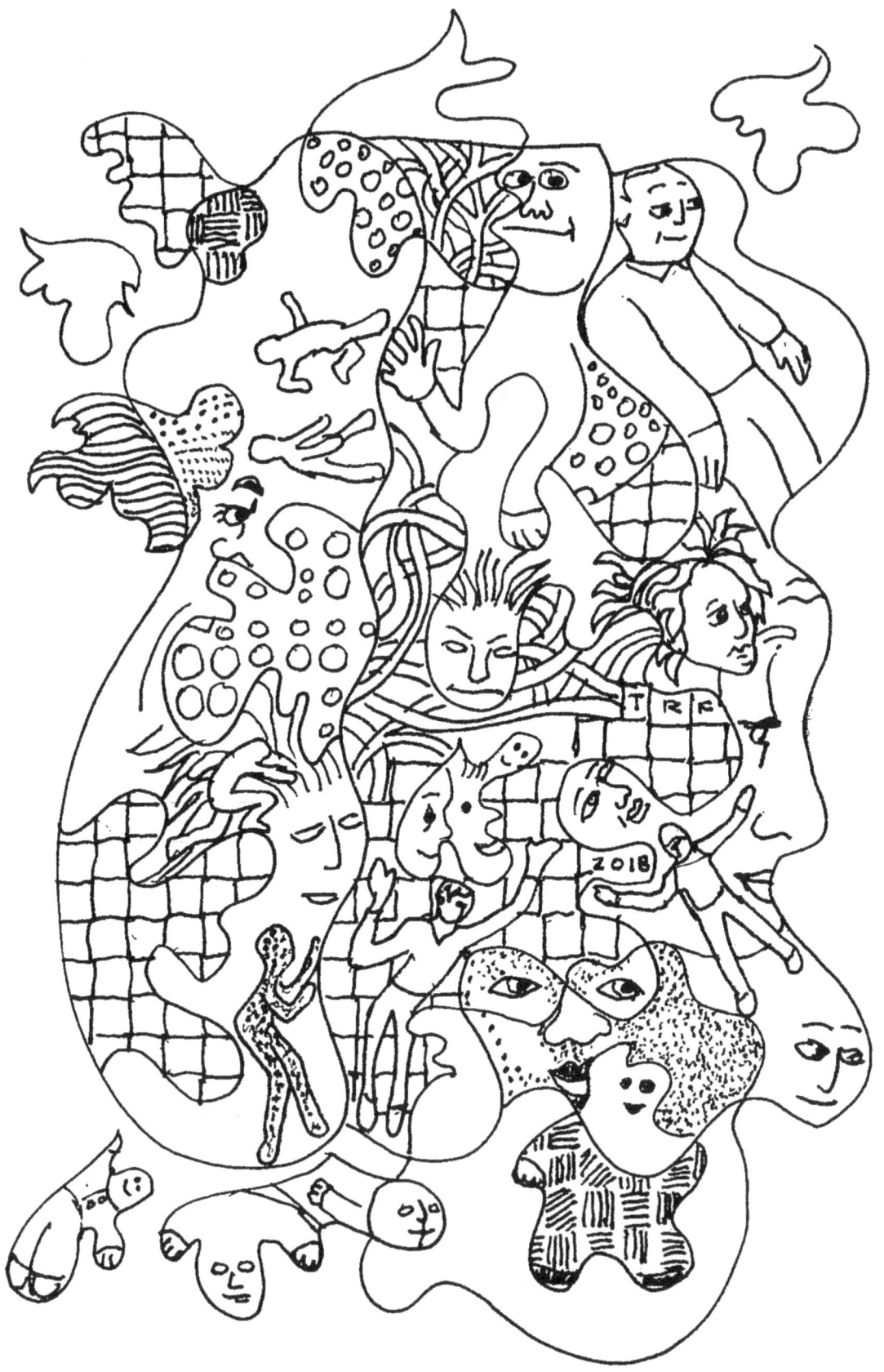

This one works pretty well
upside down....also available on
some of the garments I sell on www.Mybestthreads.com

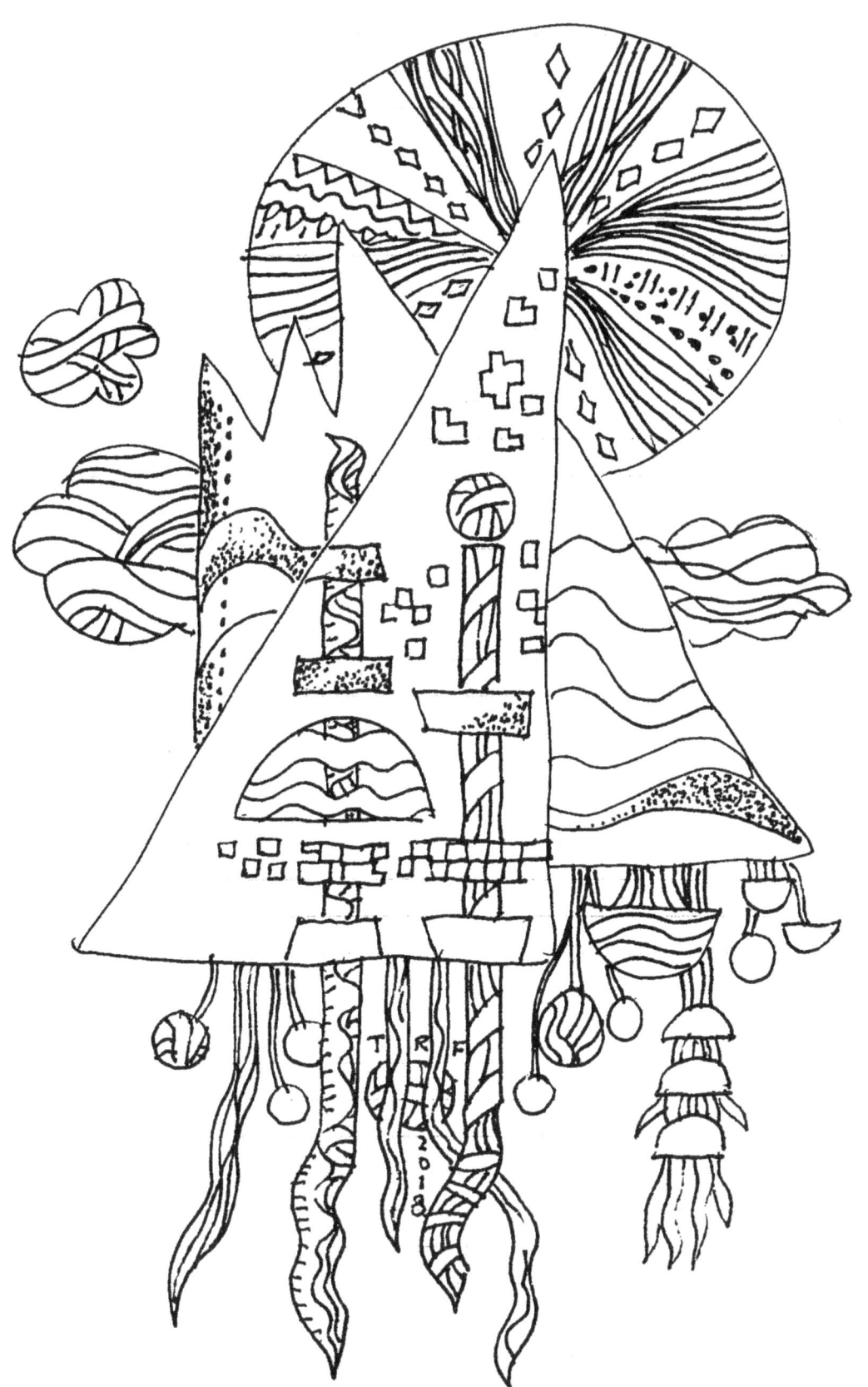

I CALL THIS ONE
"CLASH OF THE TITANS"

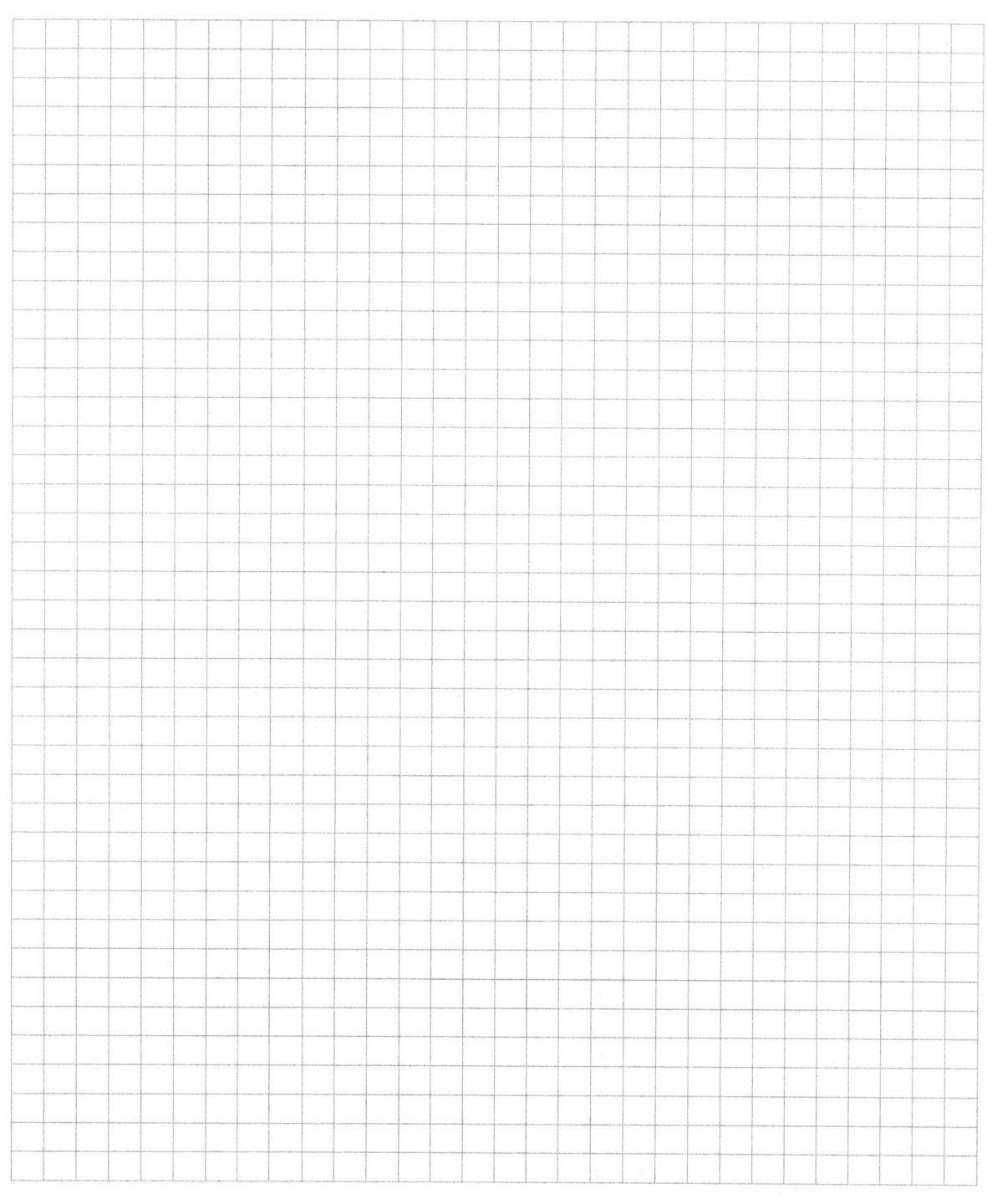

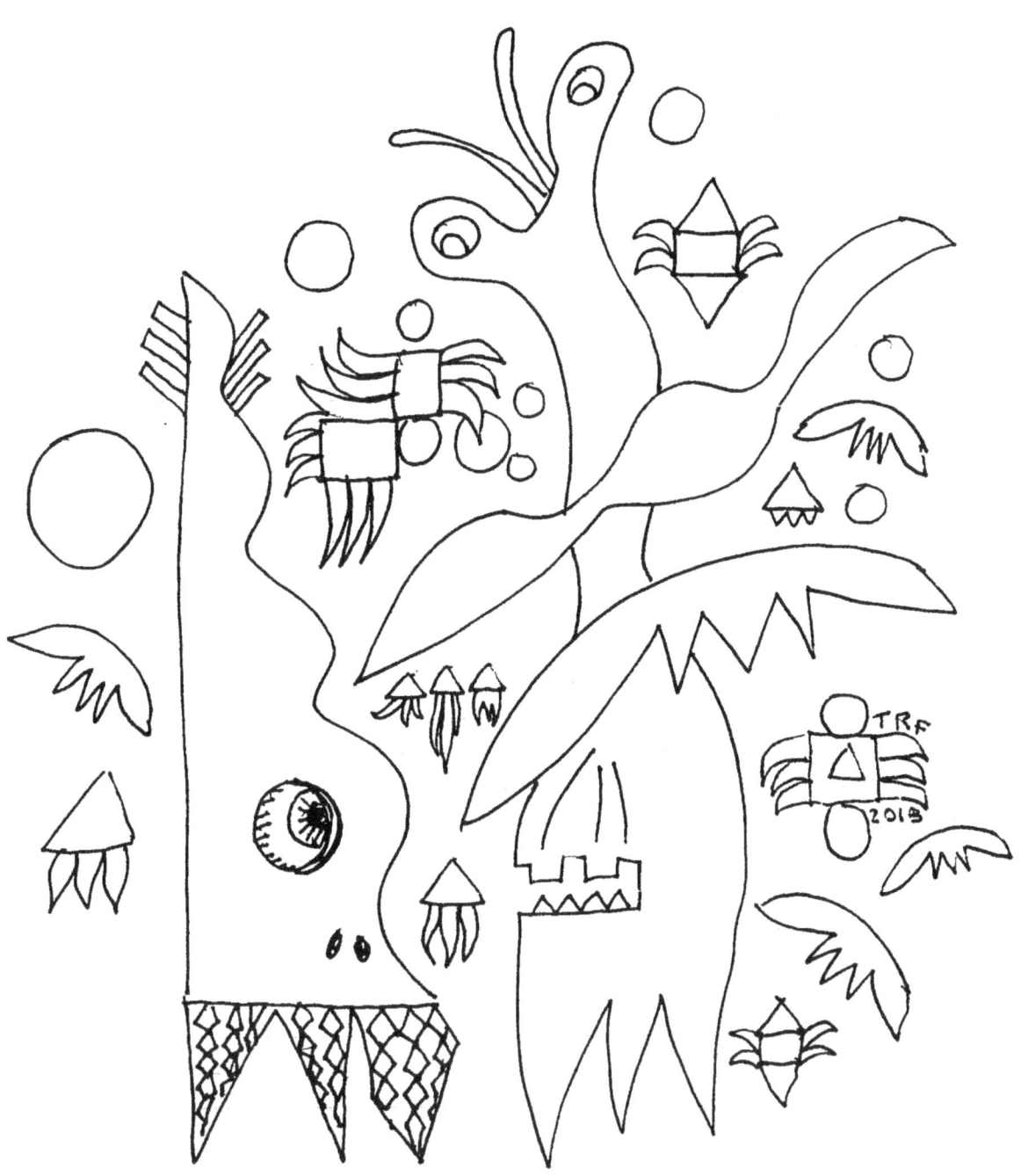

Maybe save for Halloween and use a lot of orange?

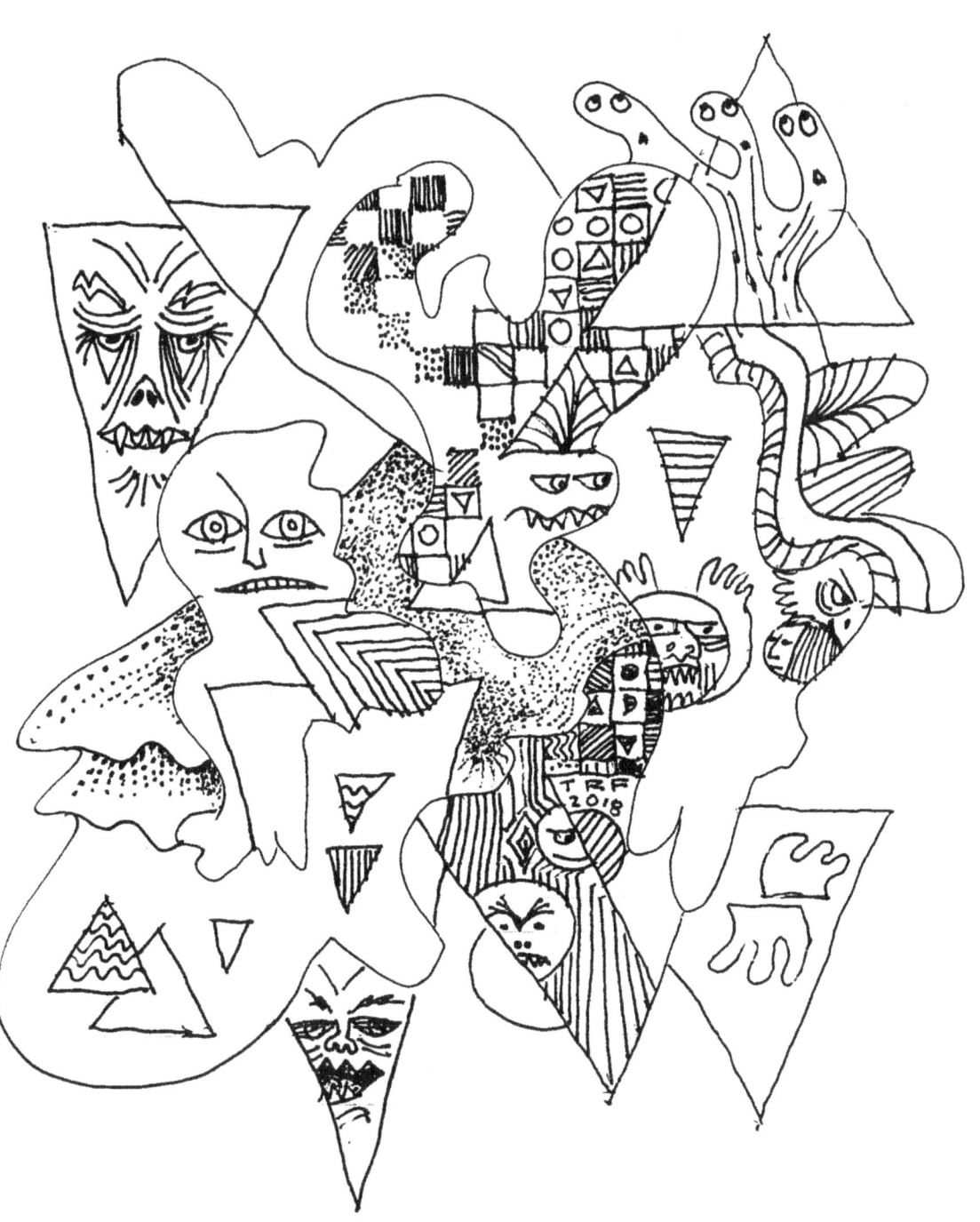

Finish this one quick!
The robots are coming.

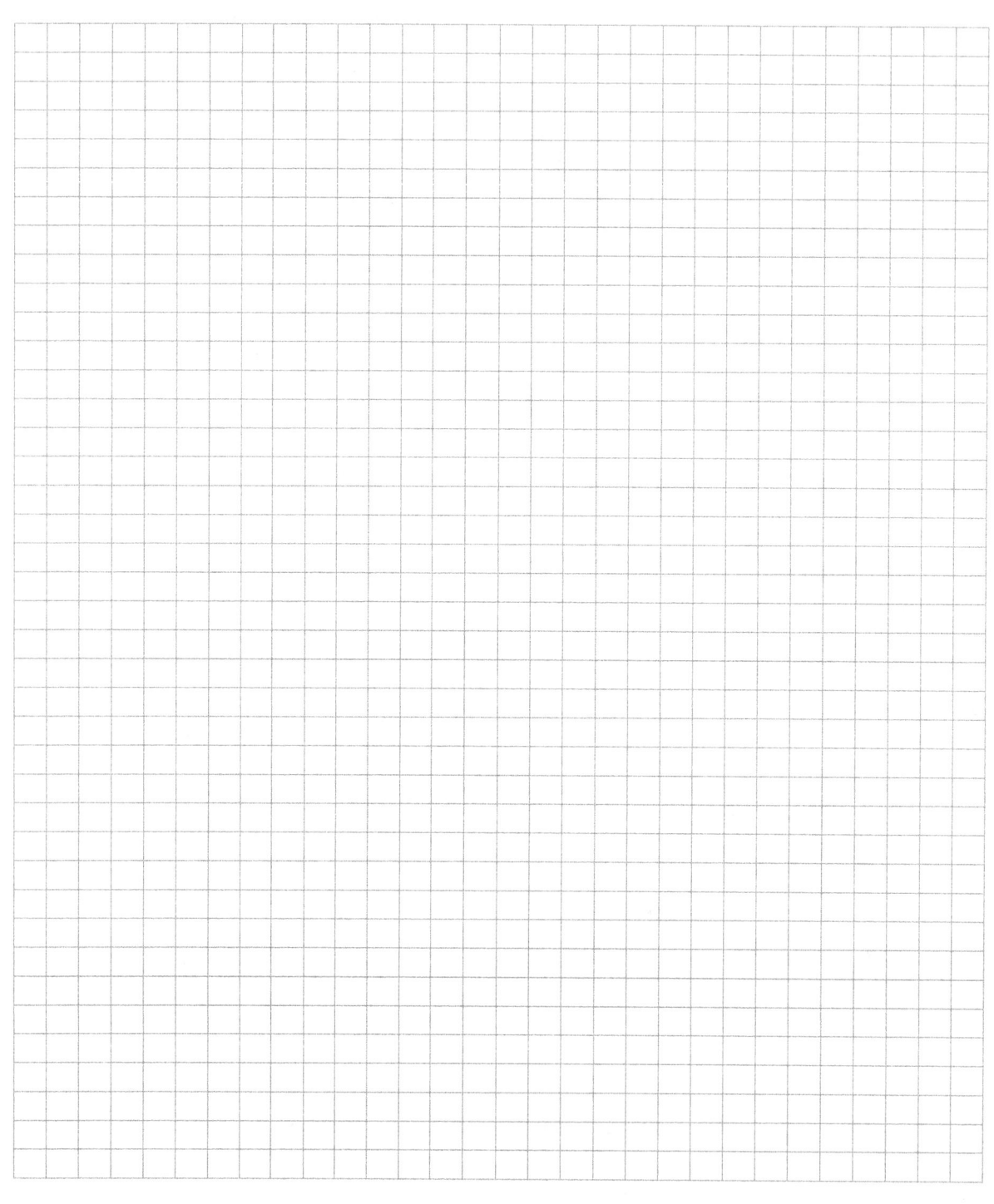

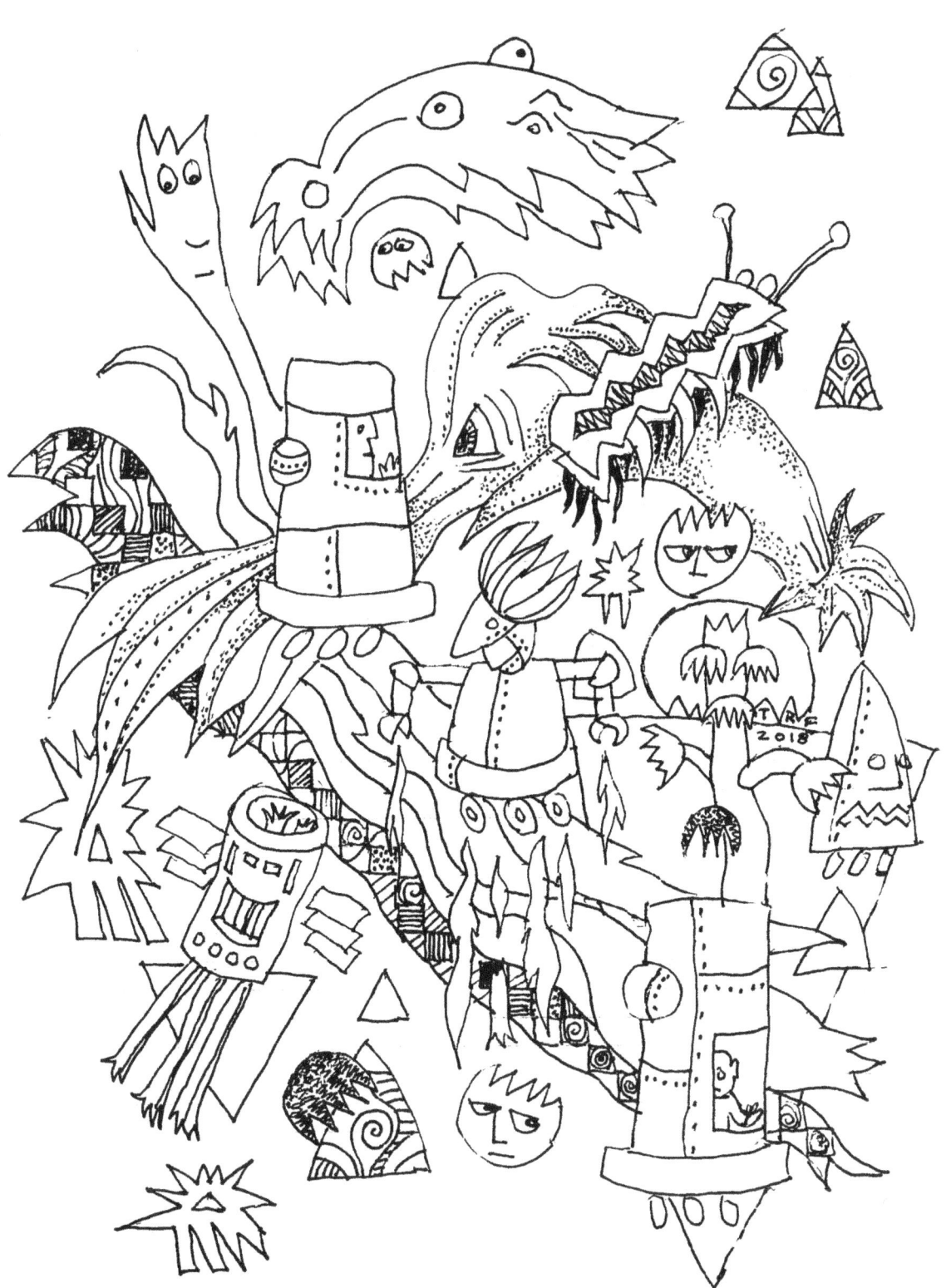

# Too much monkey business.

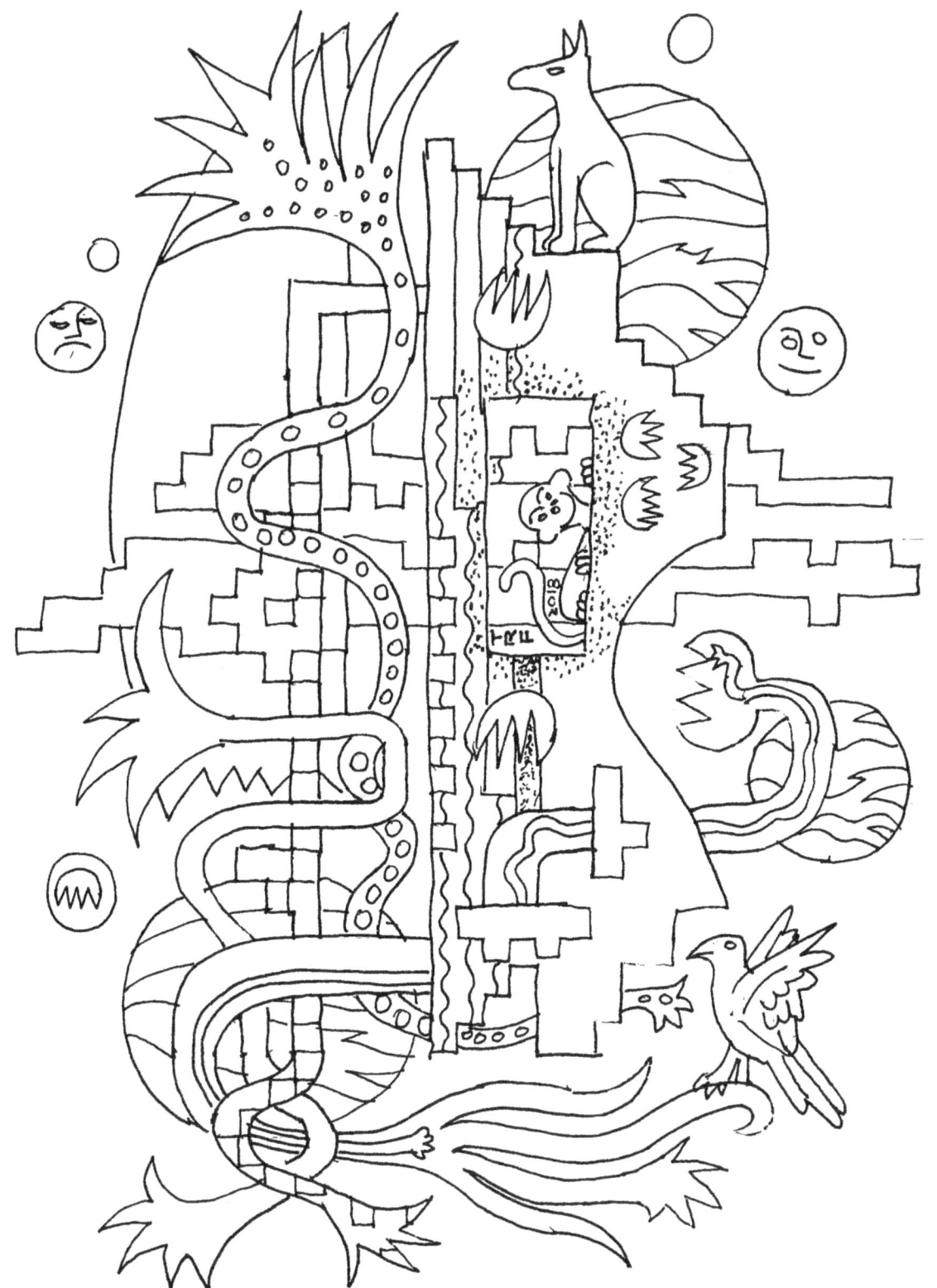

# I left some of these un-festooned to challenge you to do a little work with a black pen before you color them. (Be sure you test the black pen on another sheet of paper first and then run a color marker over it to see if it smears).

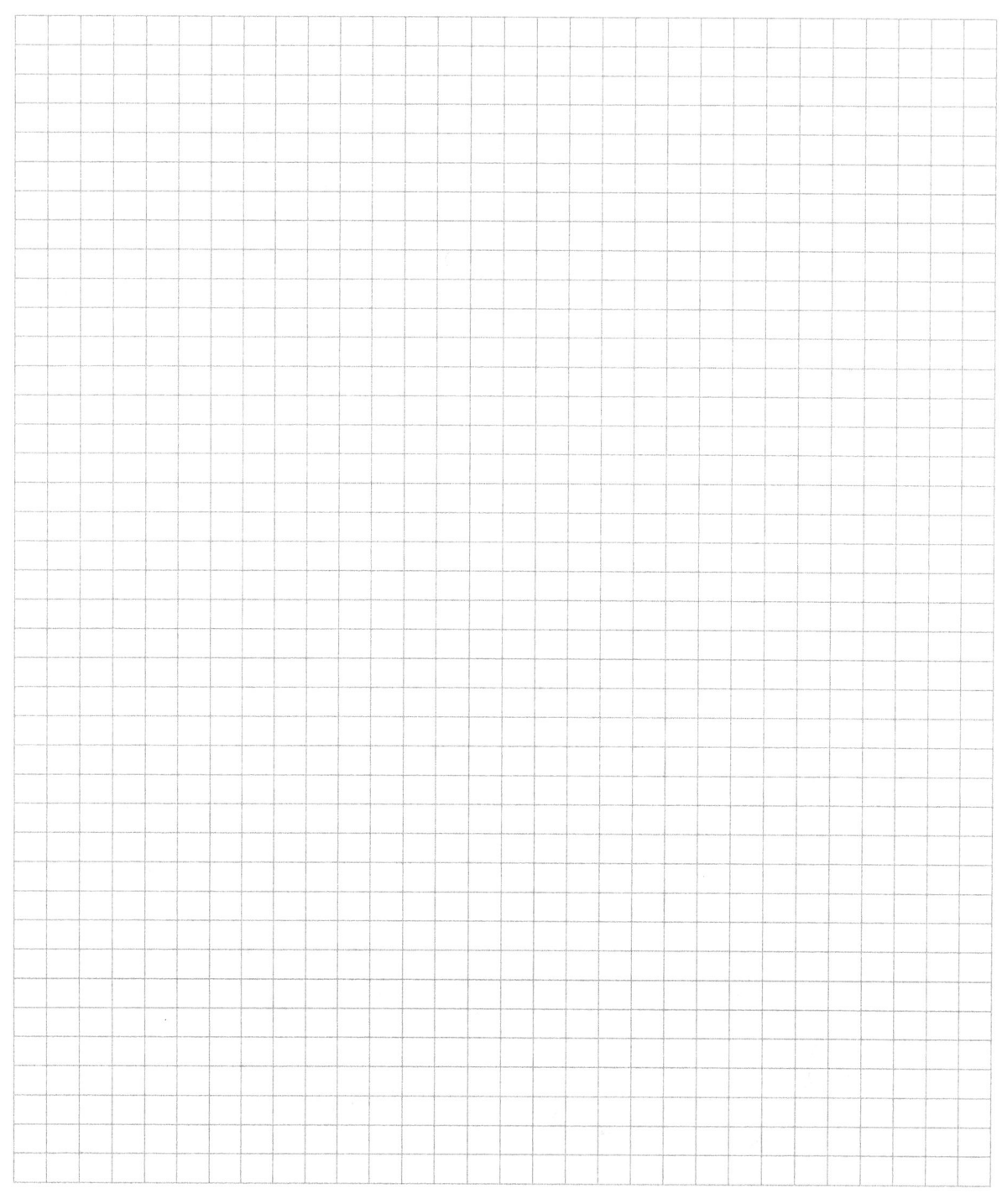

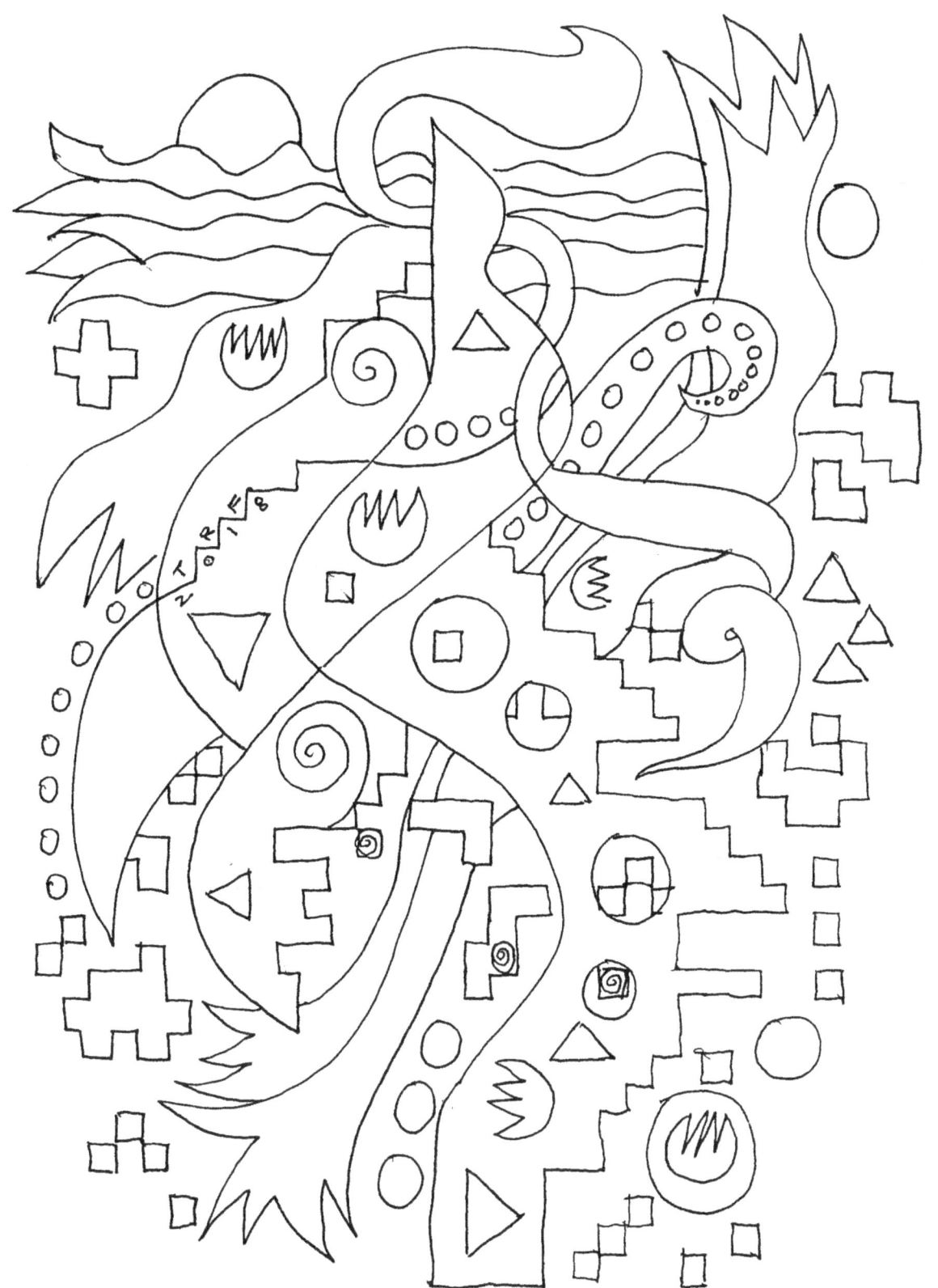

Did you look up the word "Festoon" yet?
I've been waiting for years to use it in a sentence.

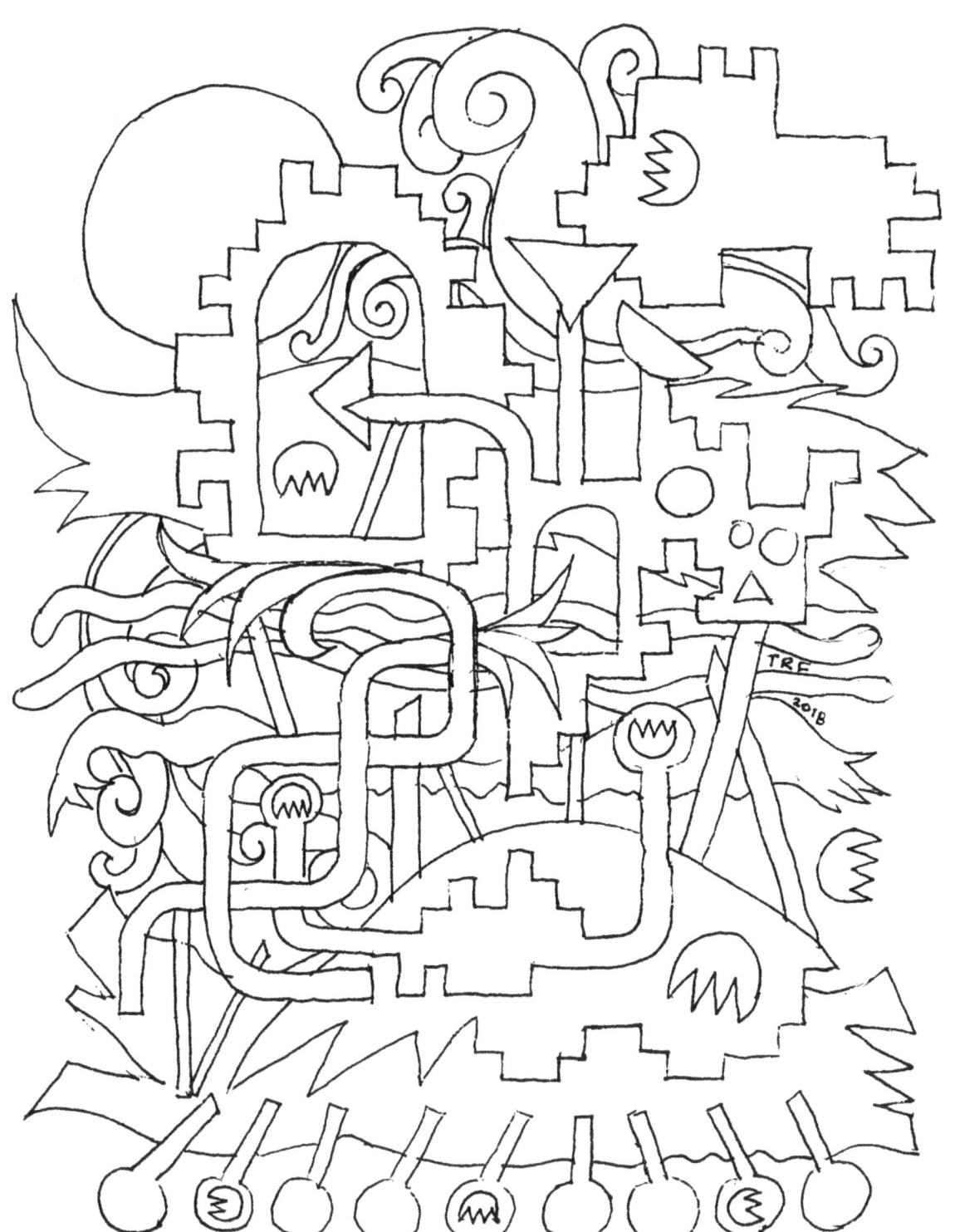

this one goes well with jazz.
Try The Steve Gadd Band - the Long Way Home

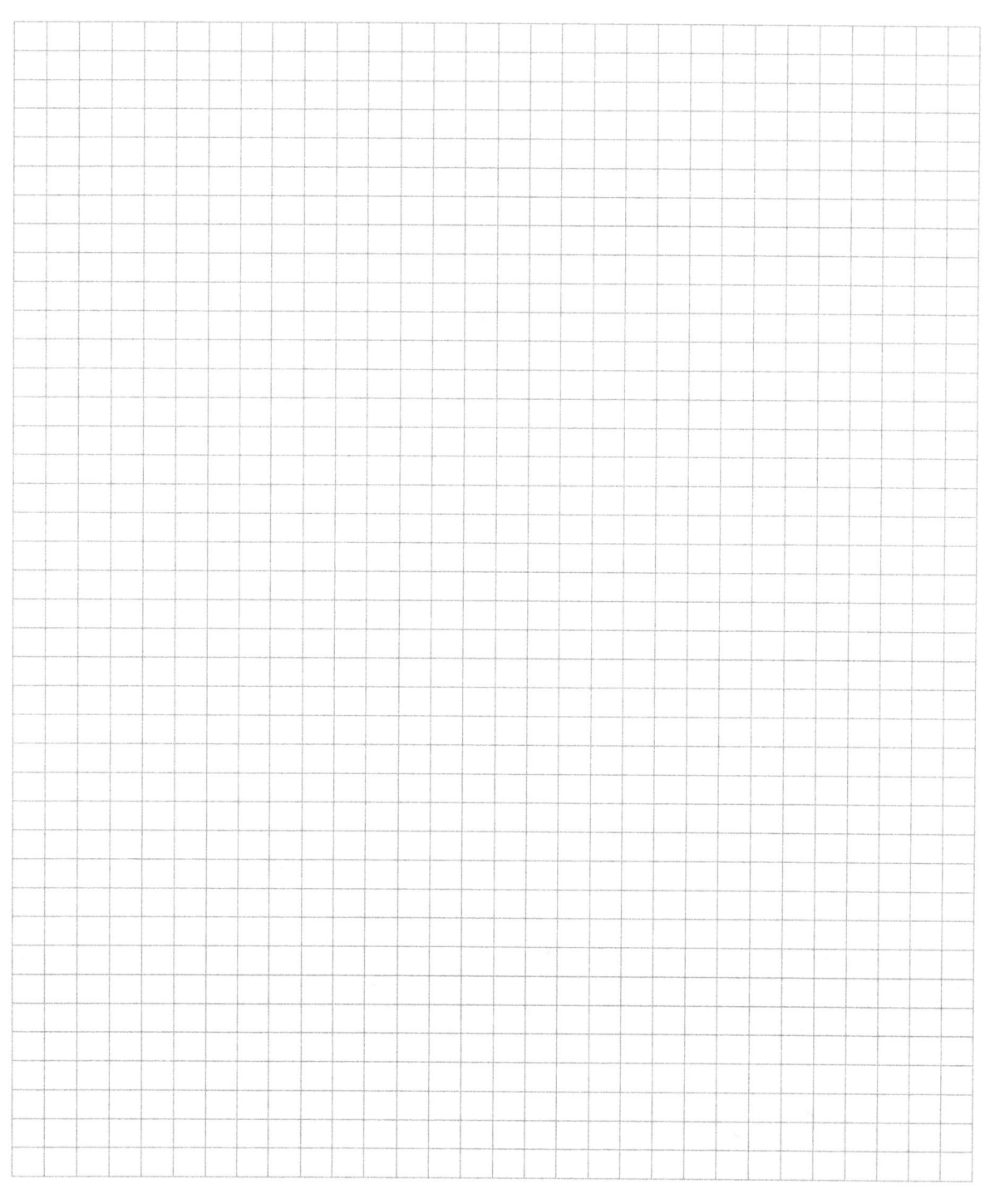

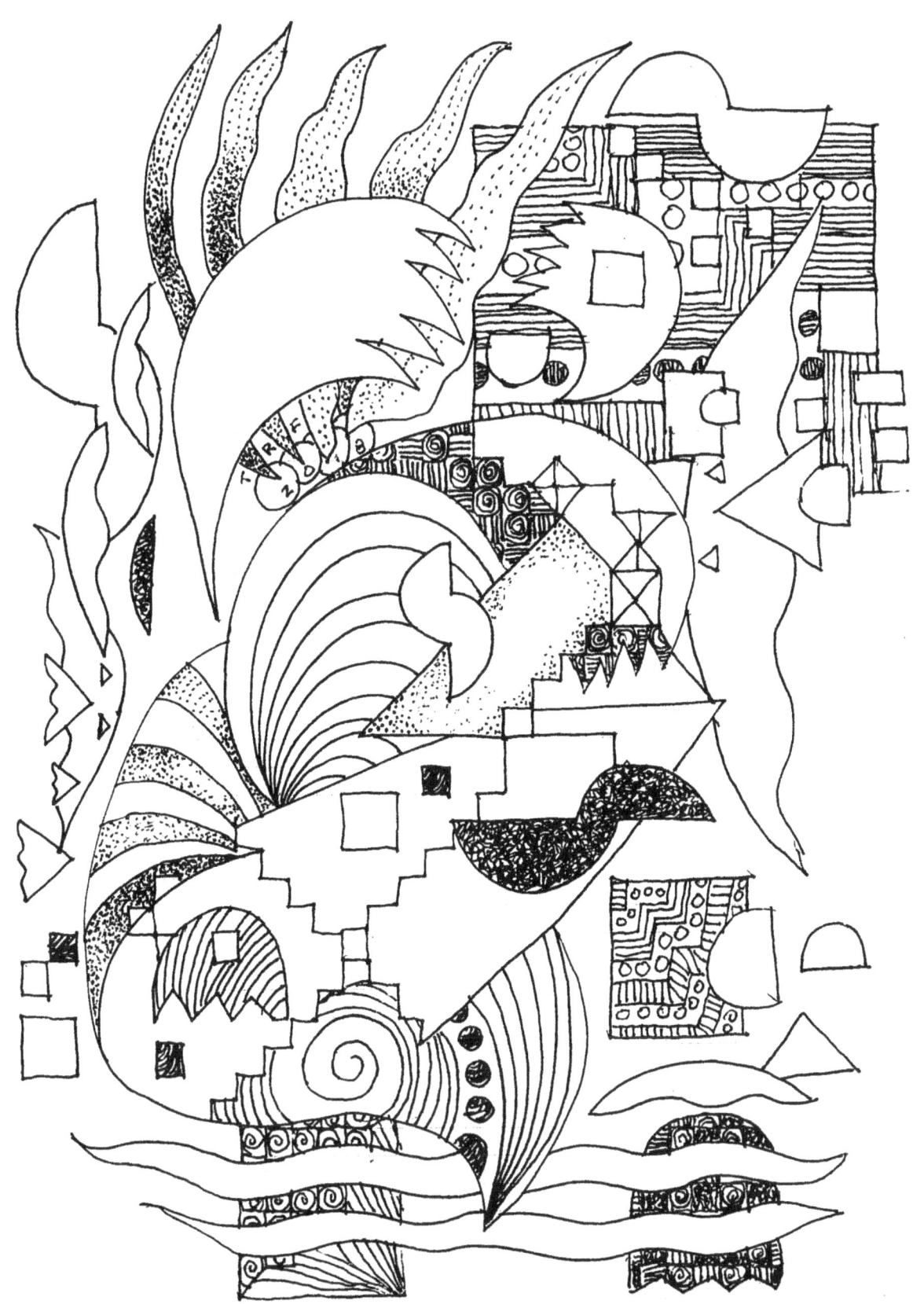

Step away from the edge.

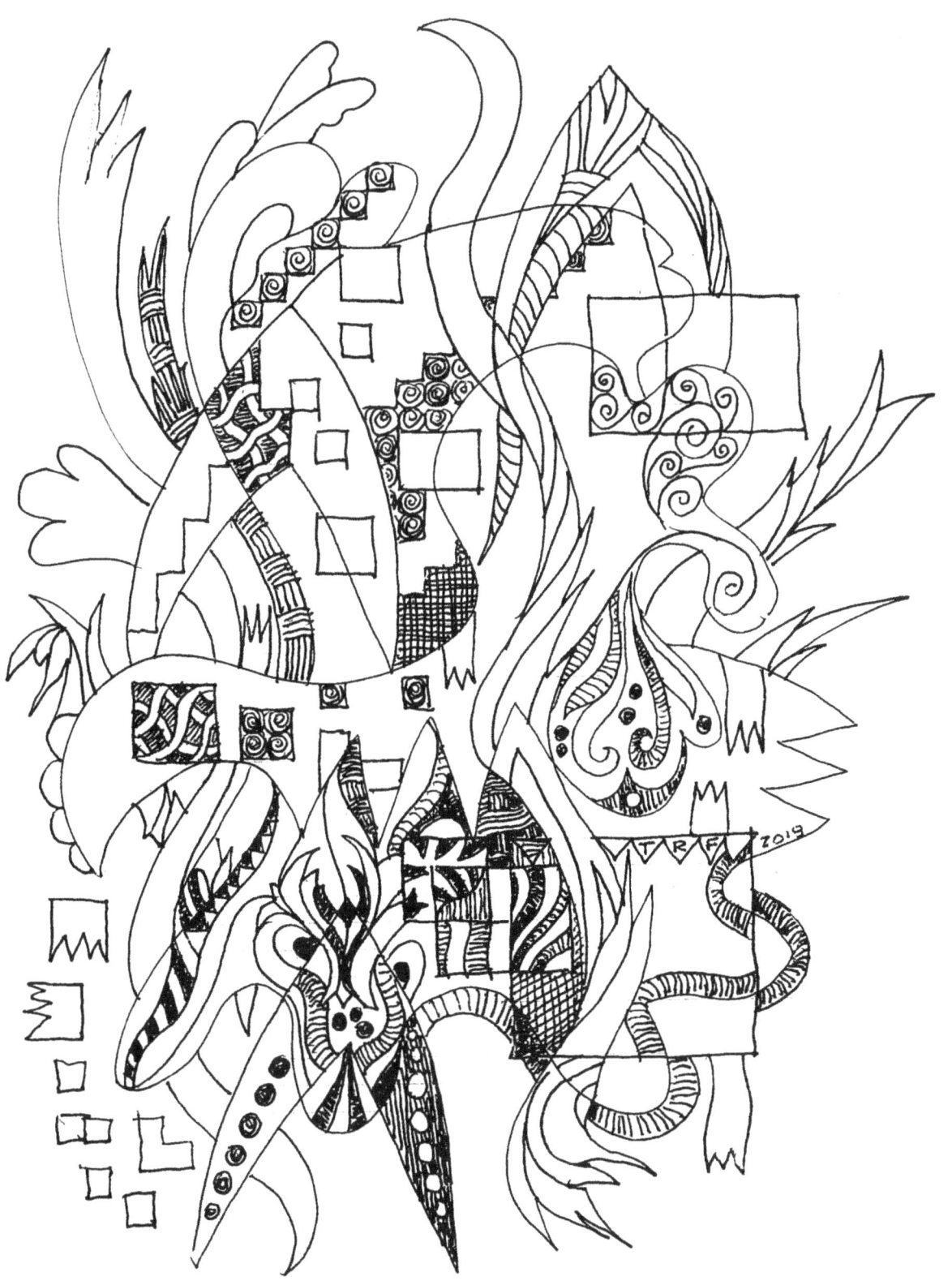

It's decision time... What color are you going to start with?

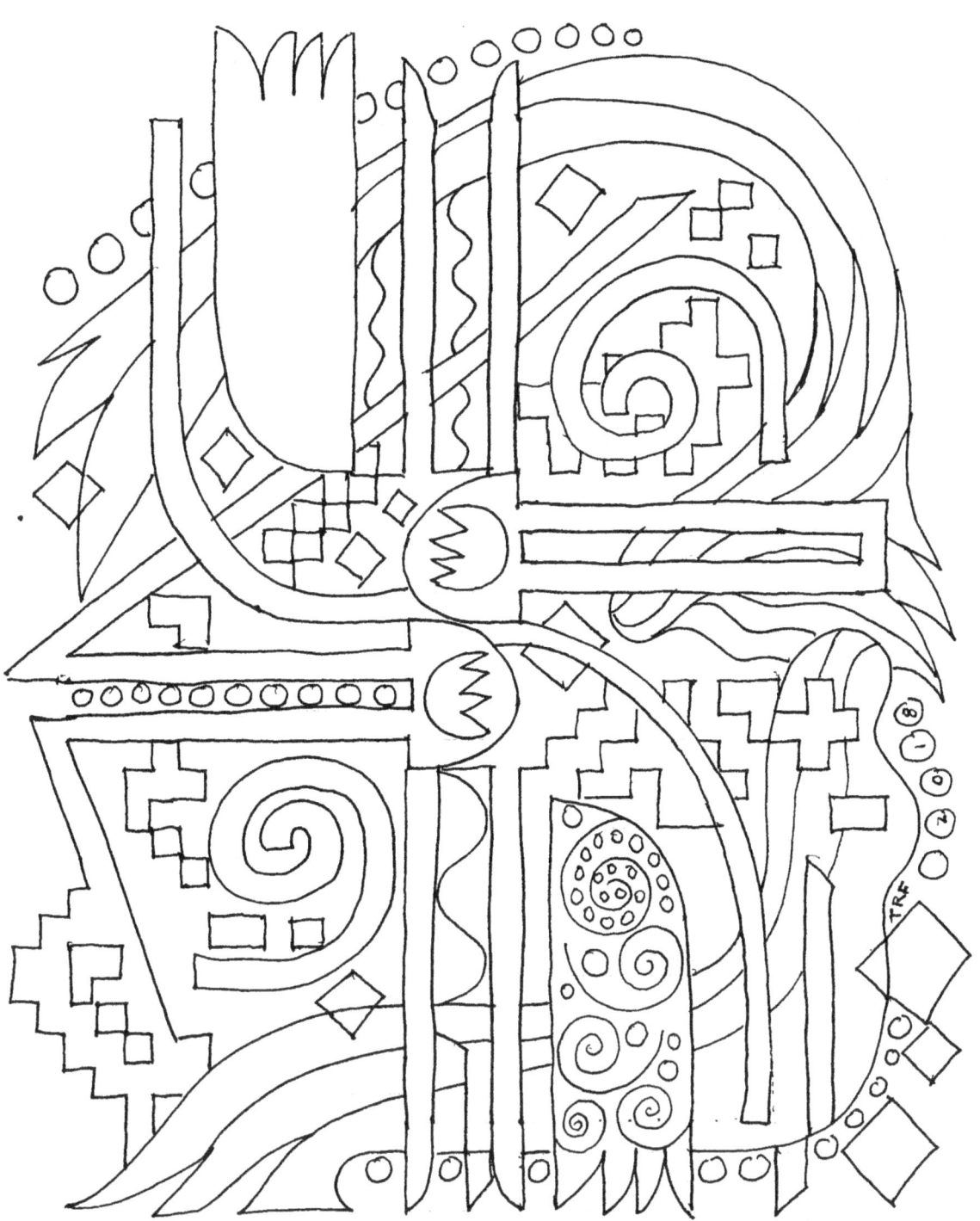

You're thinking, "Why the dinosaurs?"
Don't think, just color.

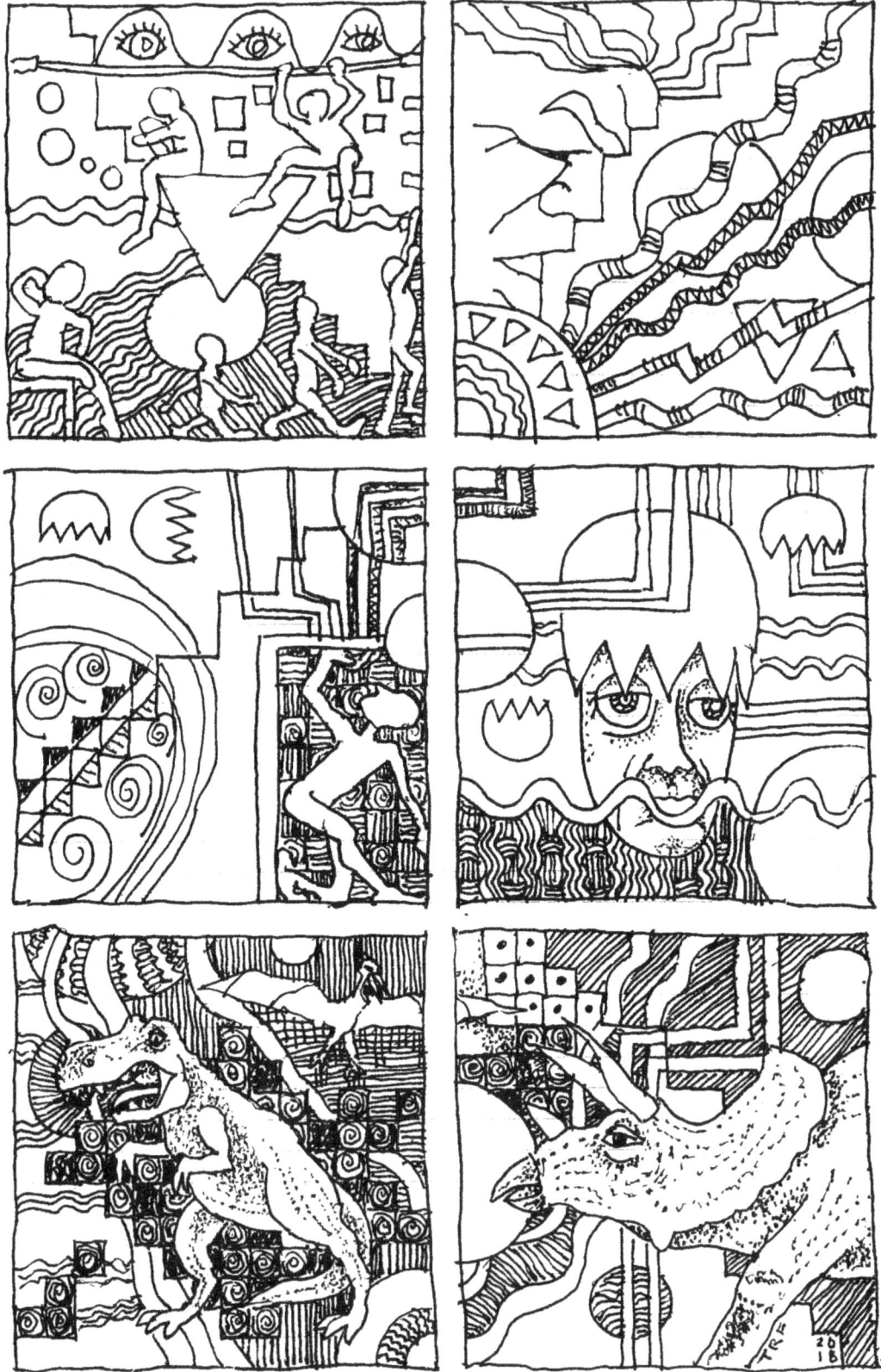

Don't get too close to the mouth...
it's the event horizon for
a black hole.

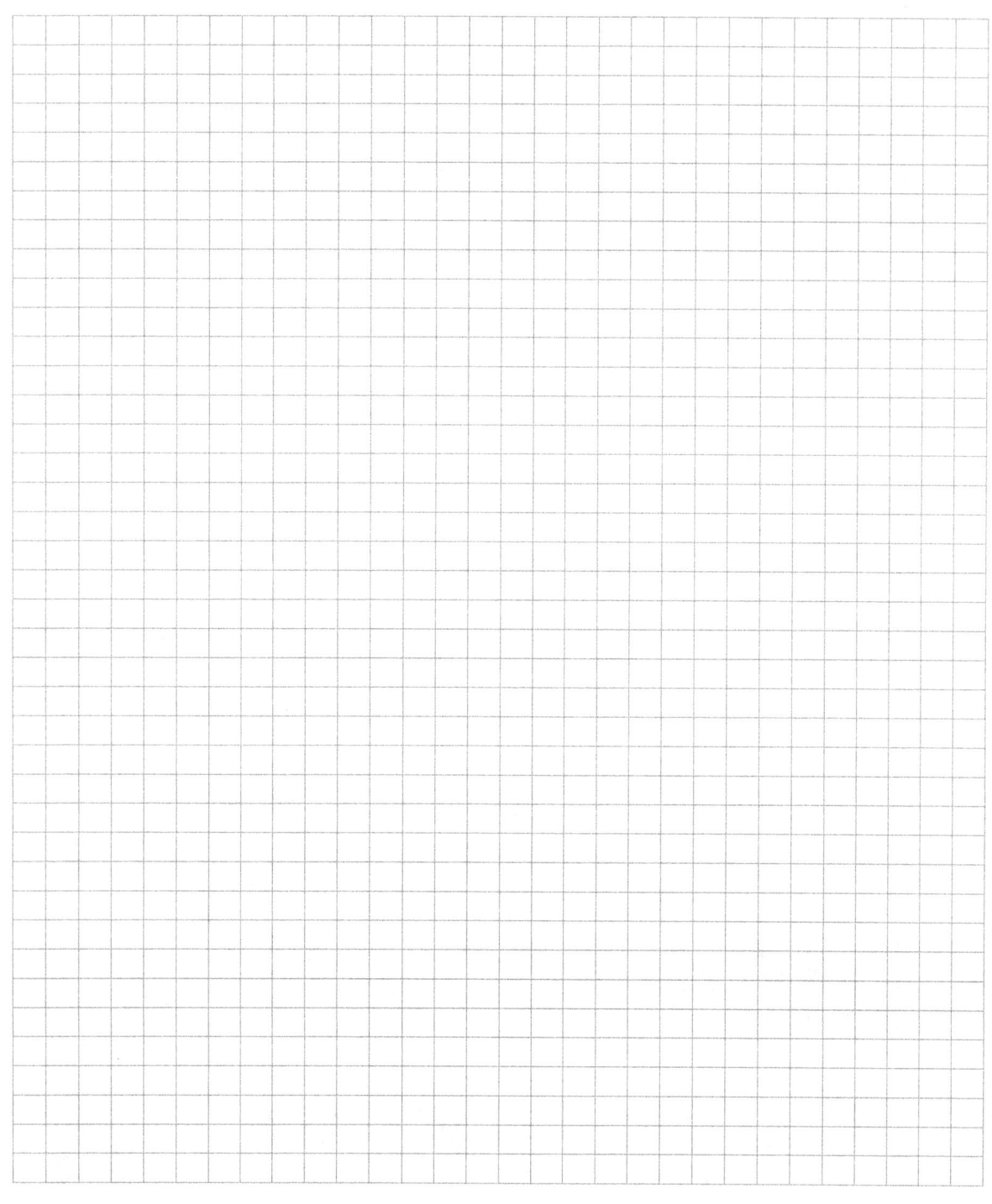

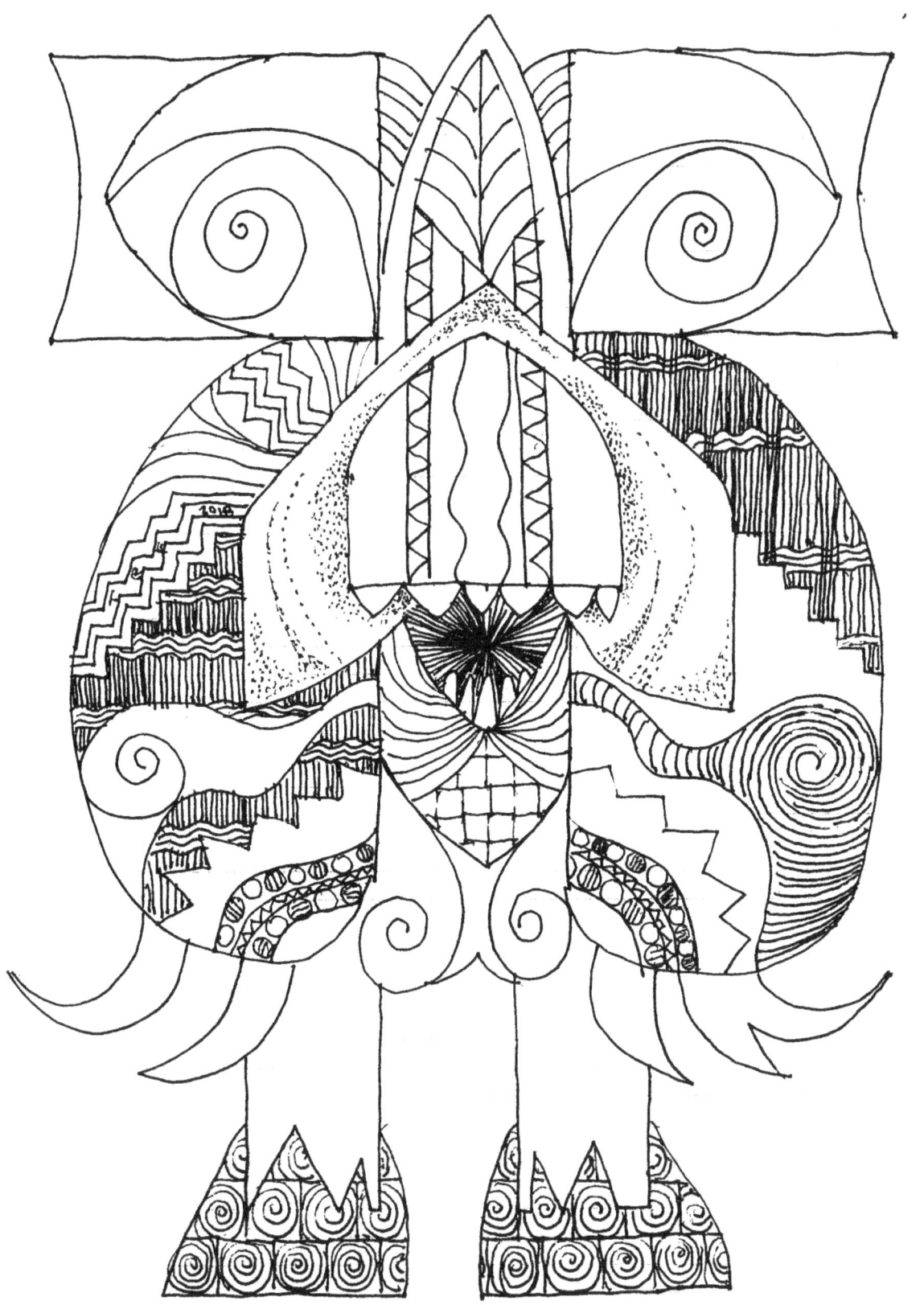

If you want to have a friend,
You gotta be a friend.

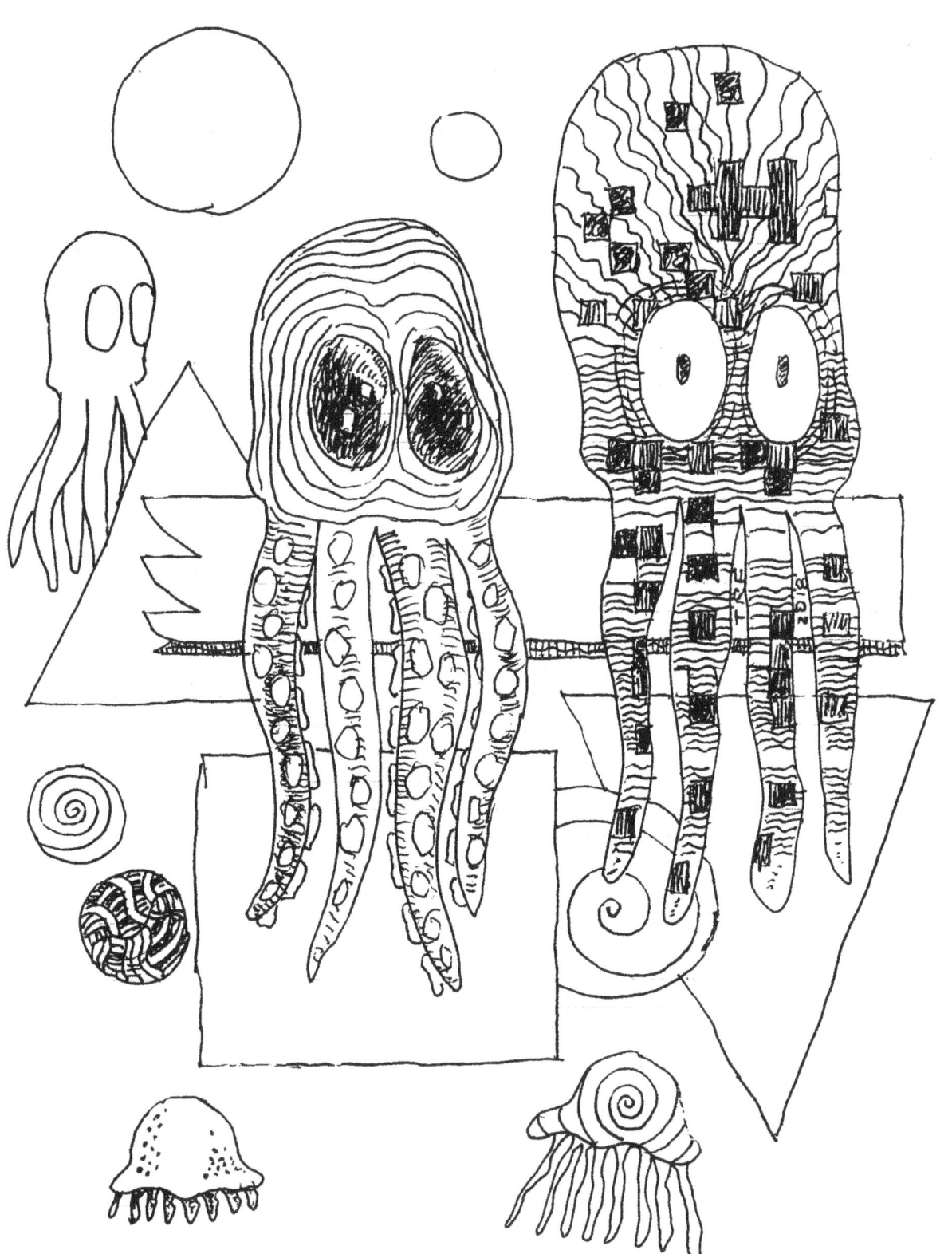

Soldier on.... I got eyes on you.

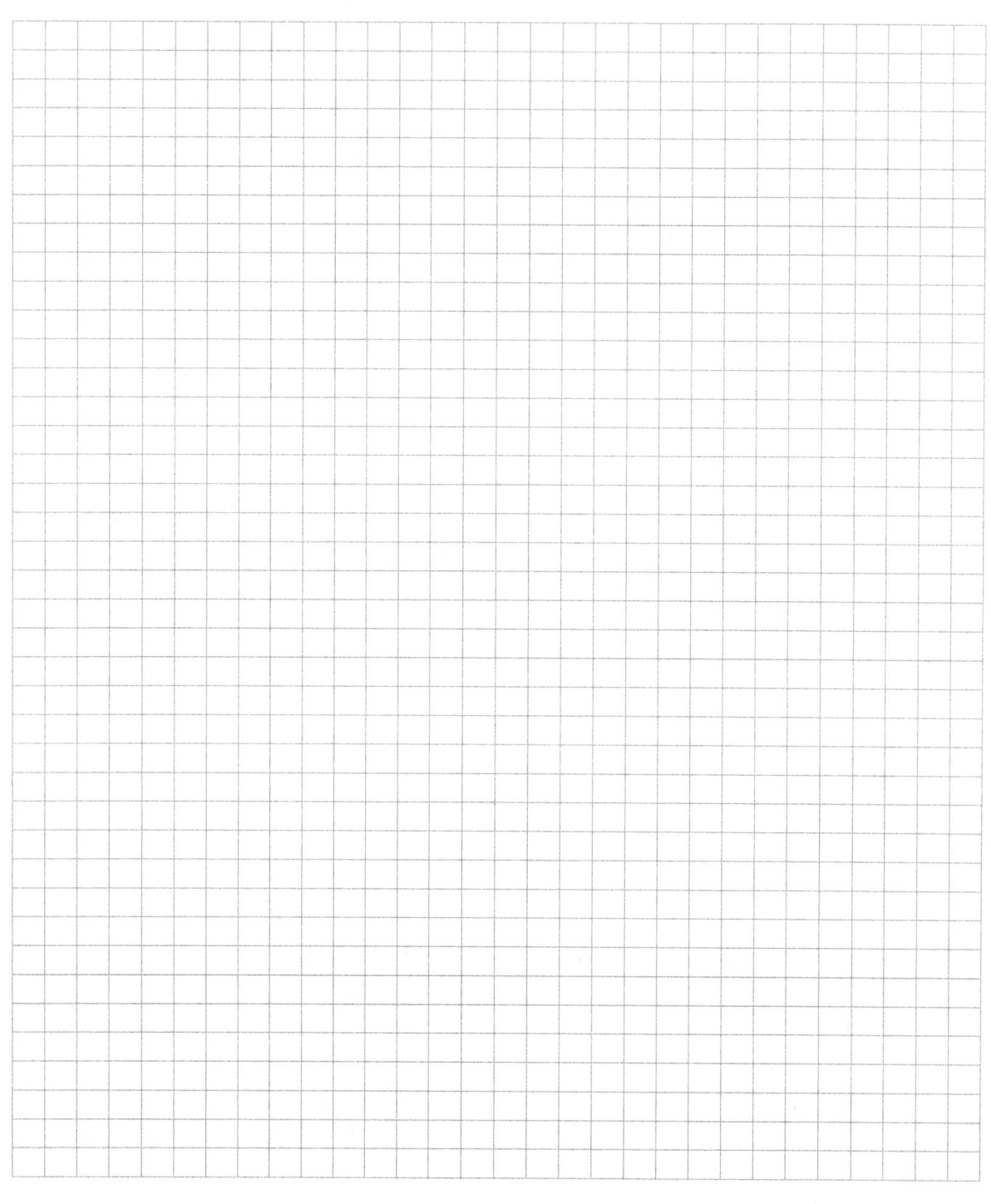

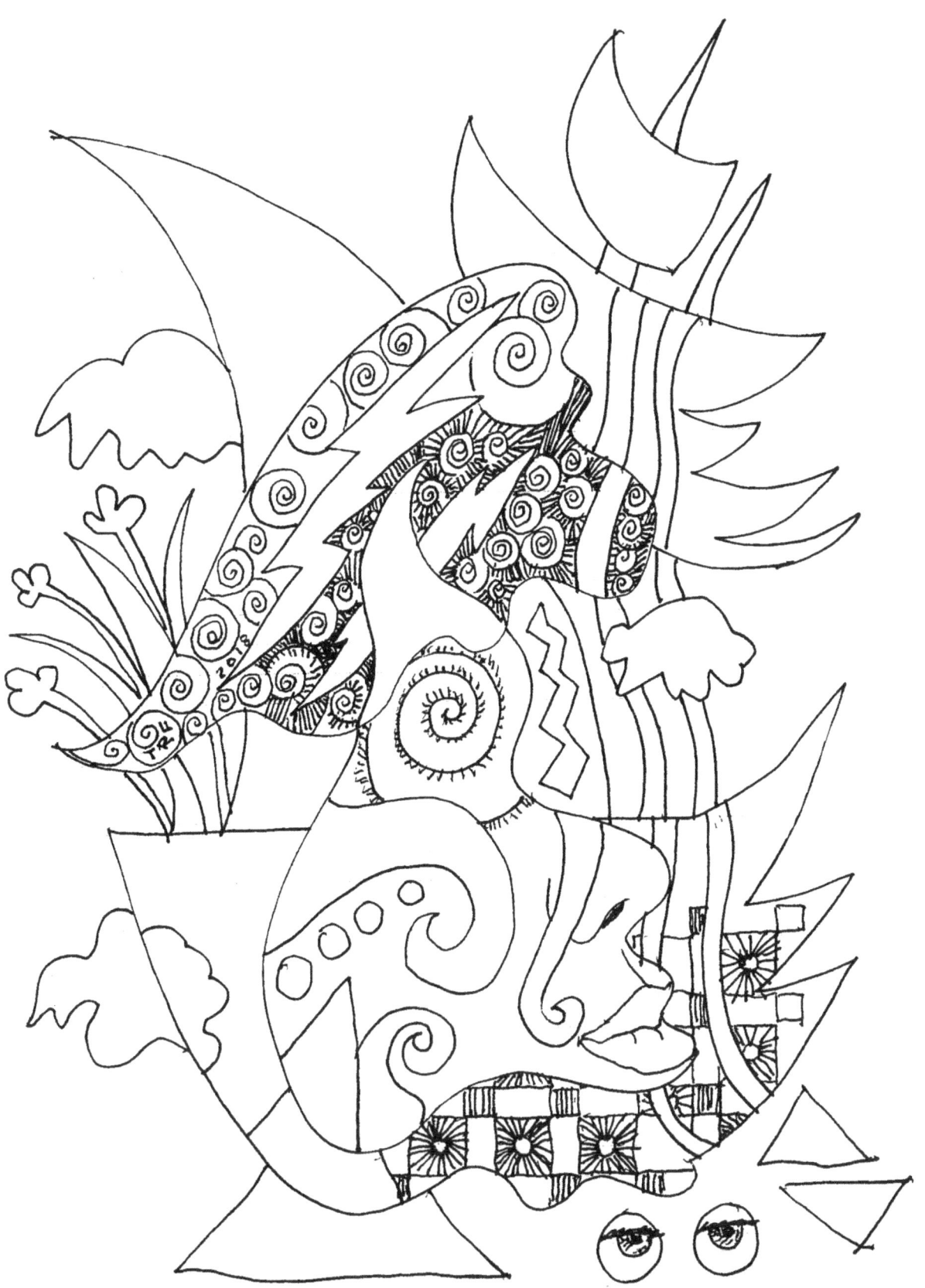

OK, you can save this for
Halloween too.

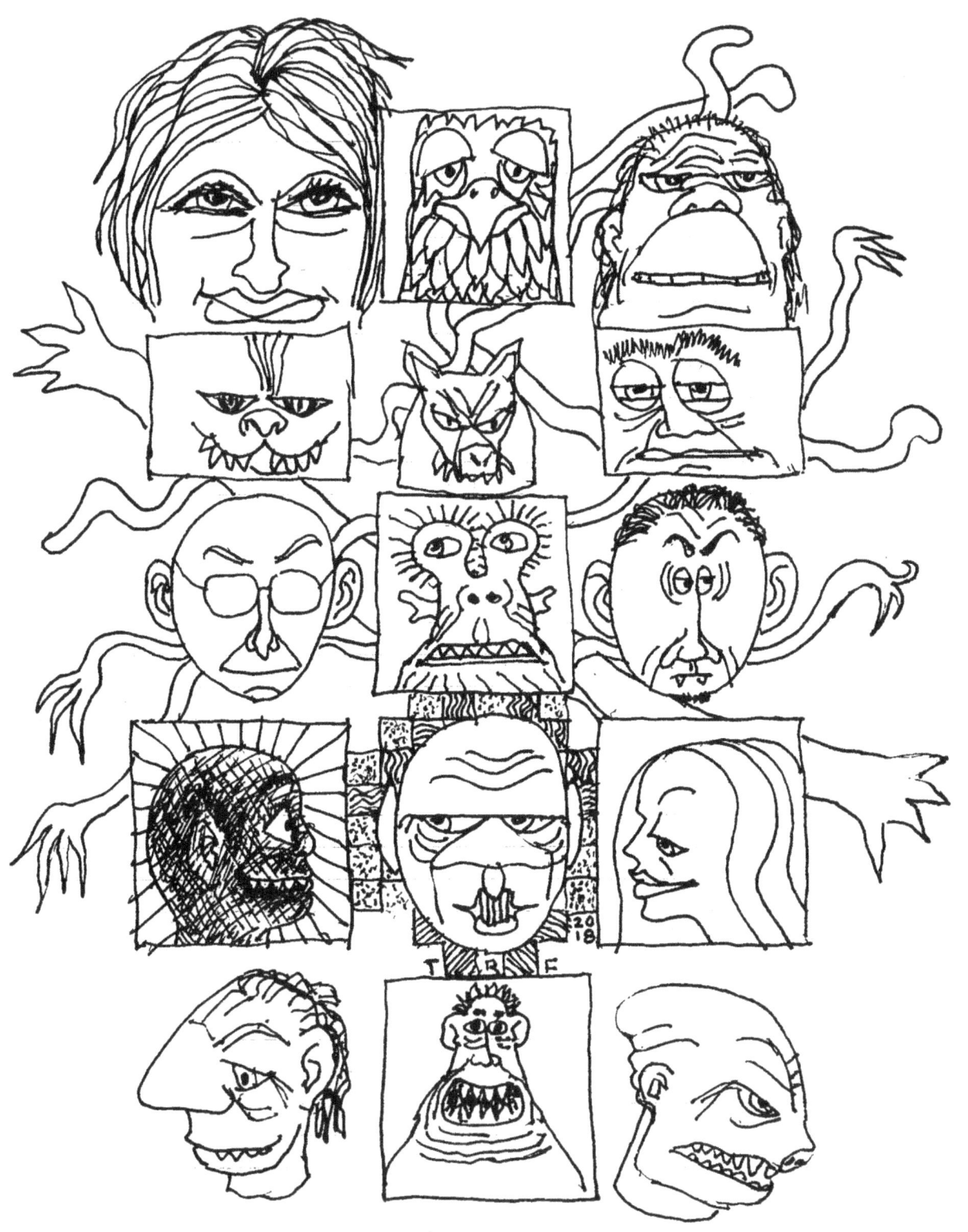

Put on some tunes, take a deep breath,
Let it out real SLOW...
Now color.

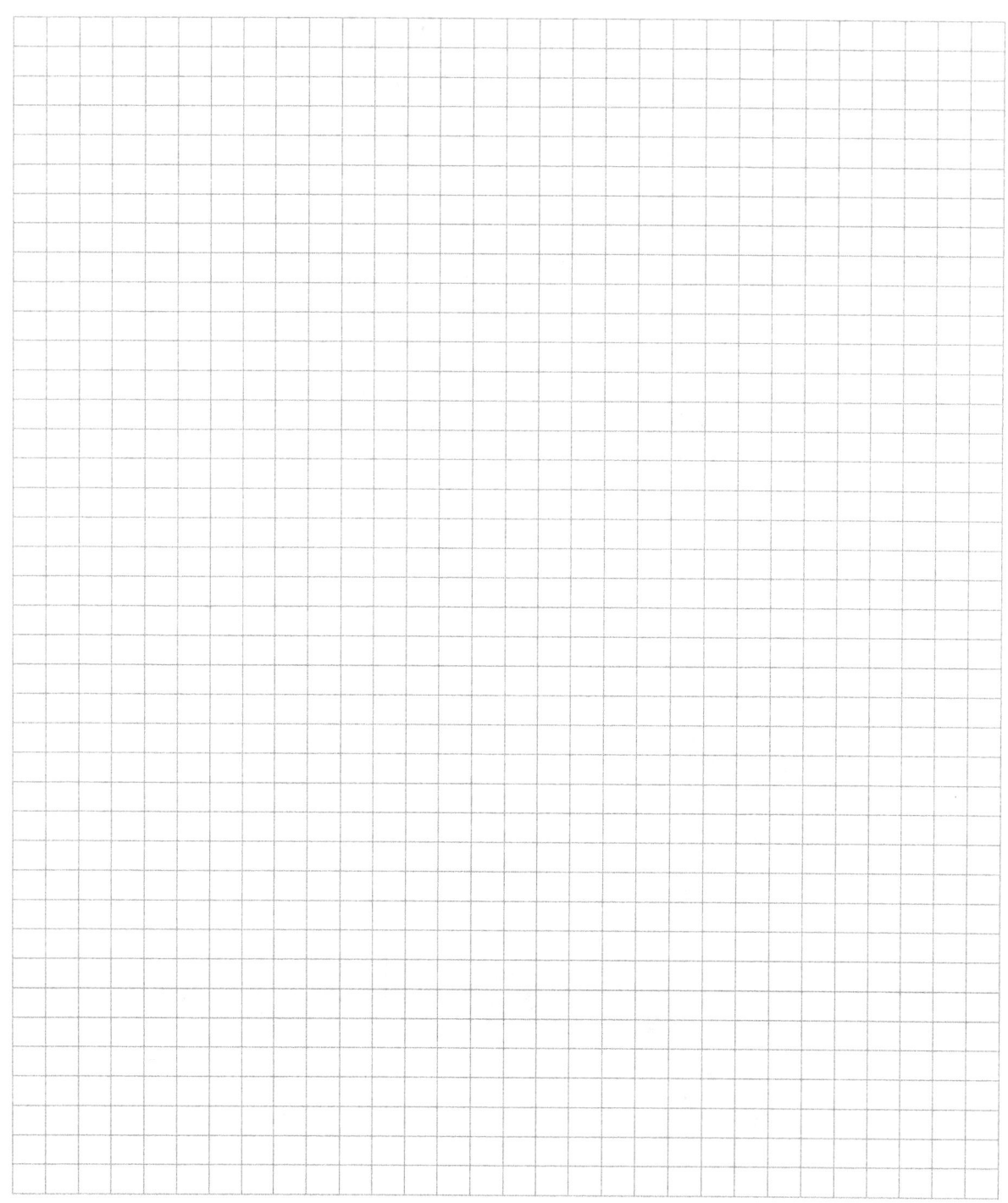

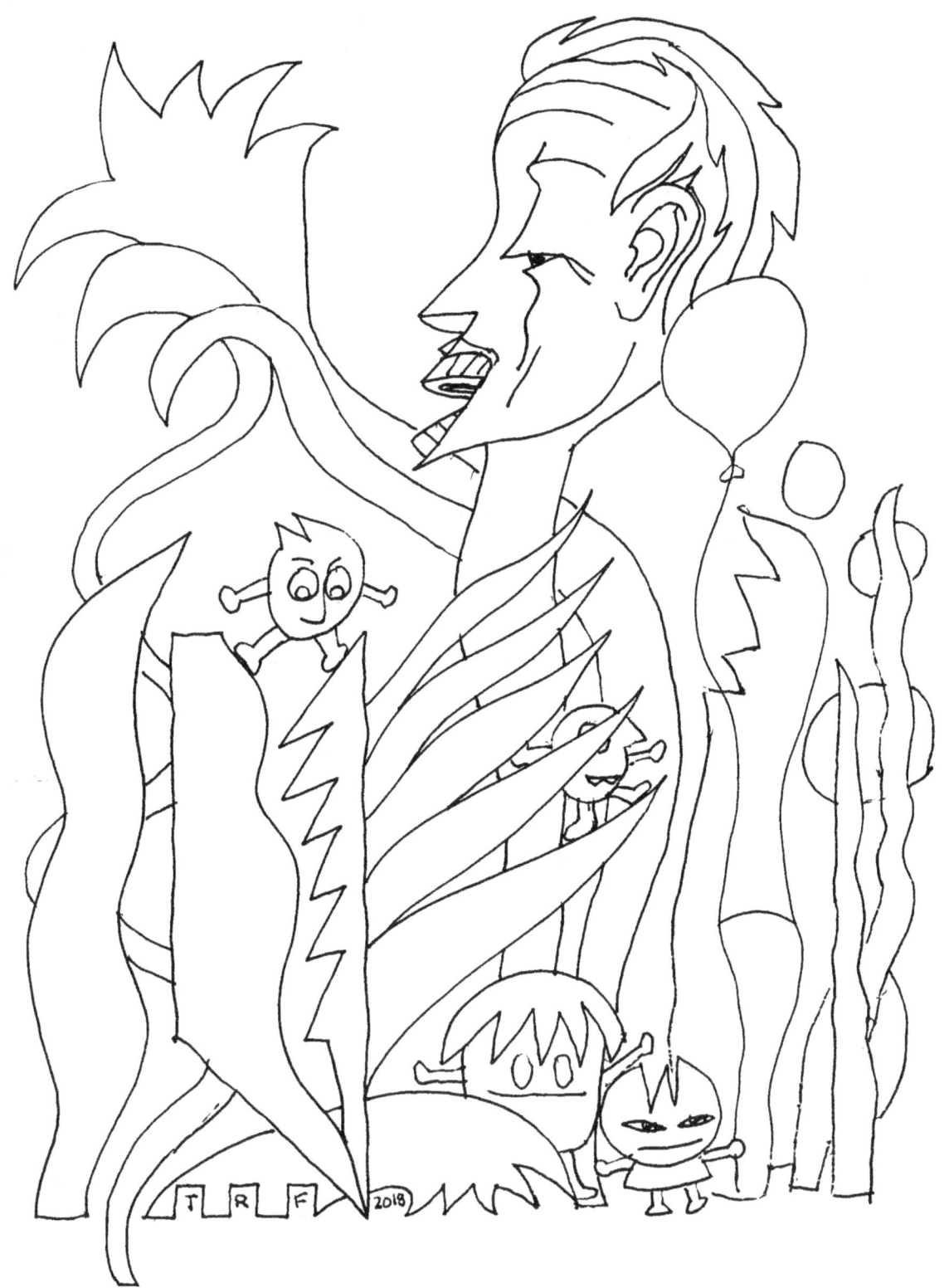

Hey, I left you some room to add a little color, quit whining!

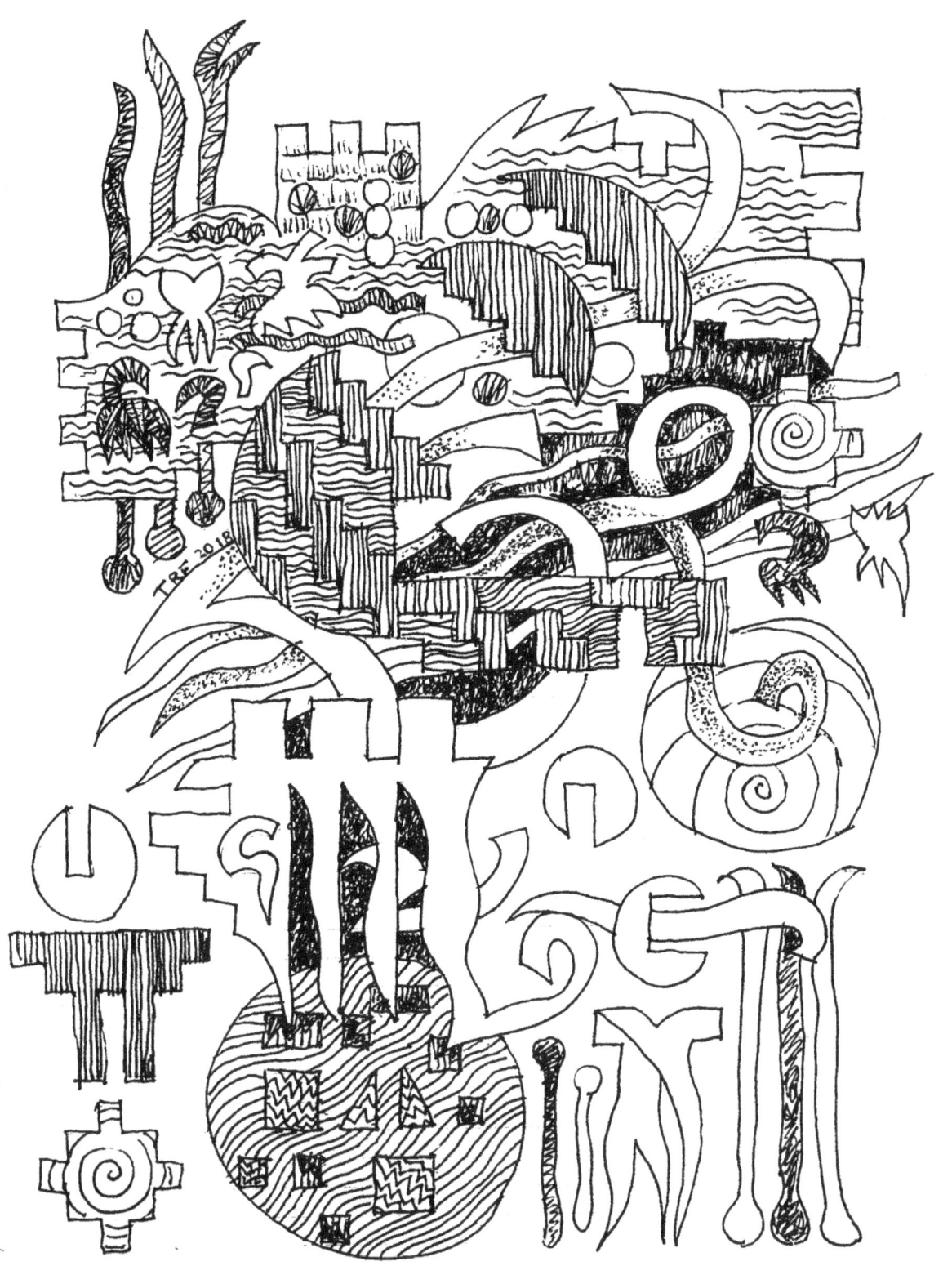

Does something about this drawing bug you?

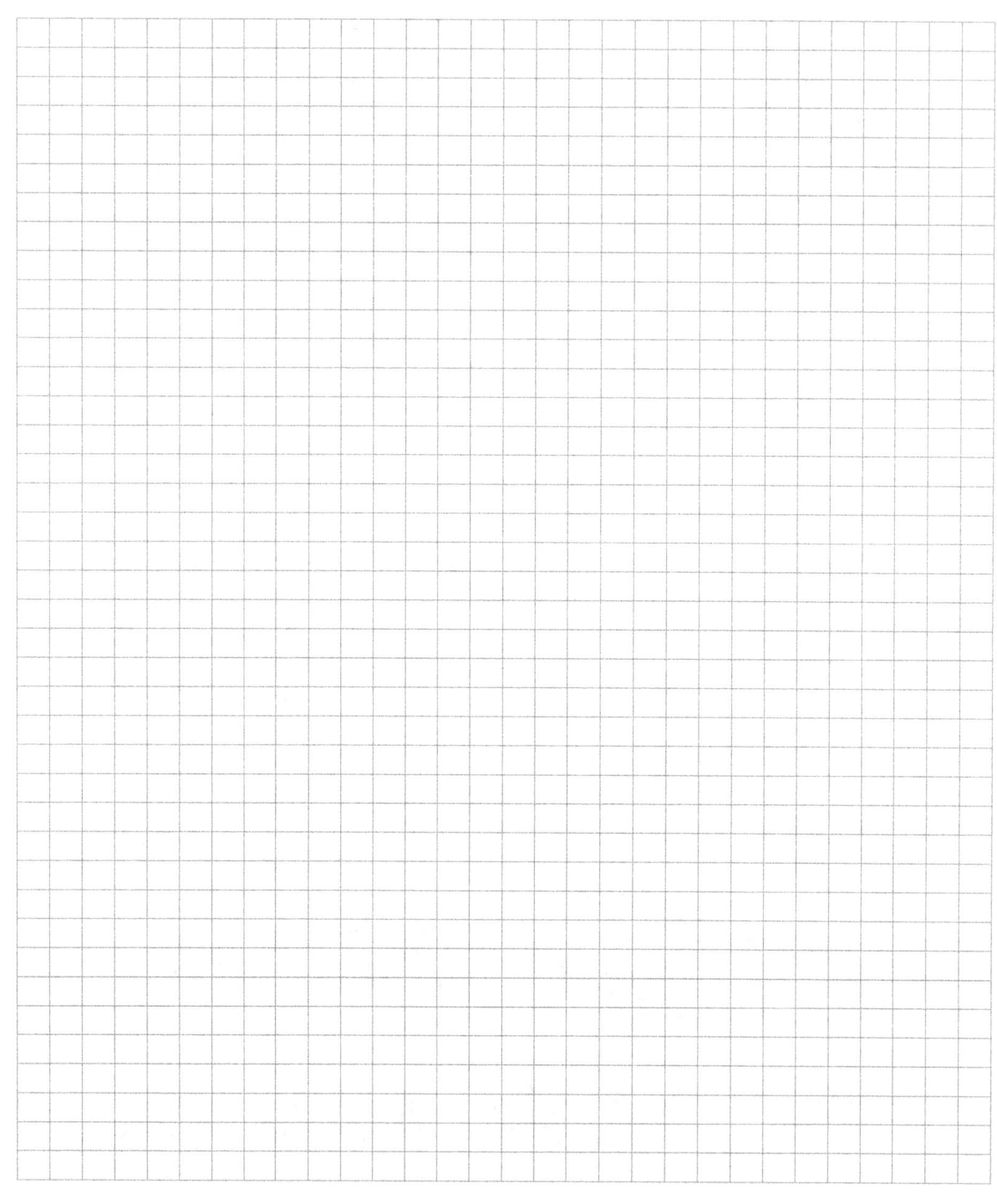

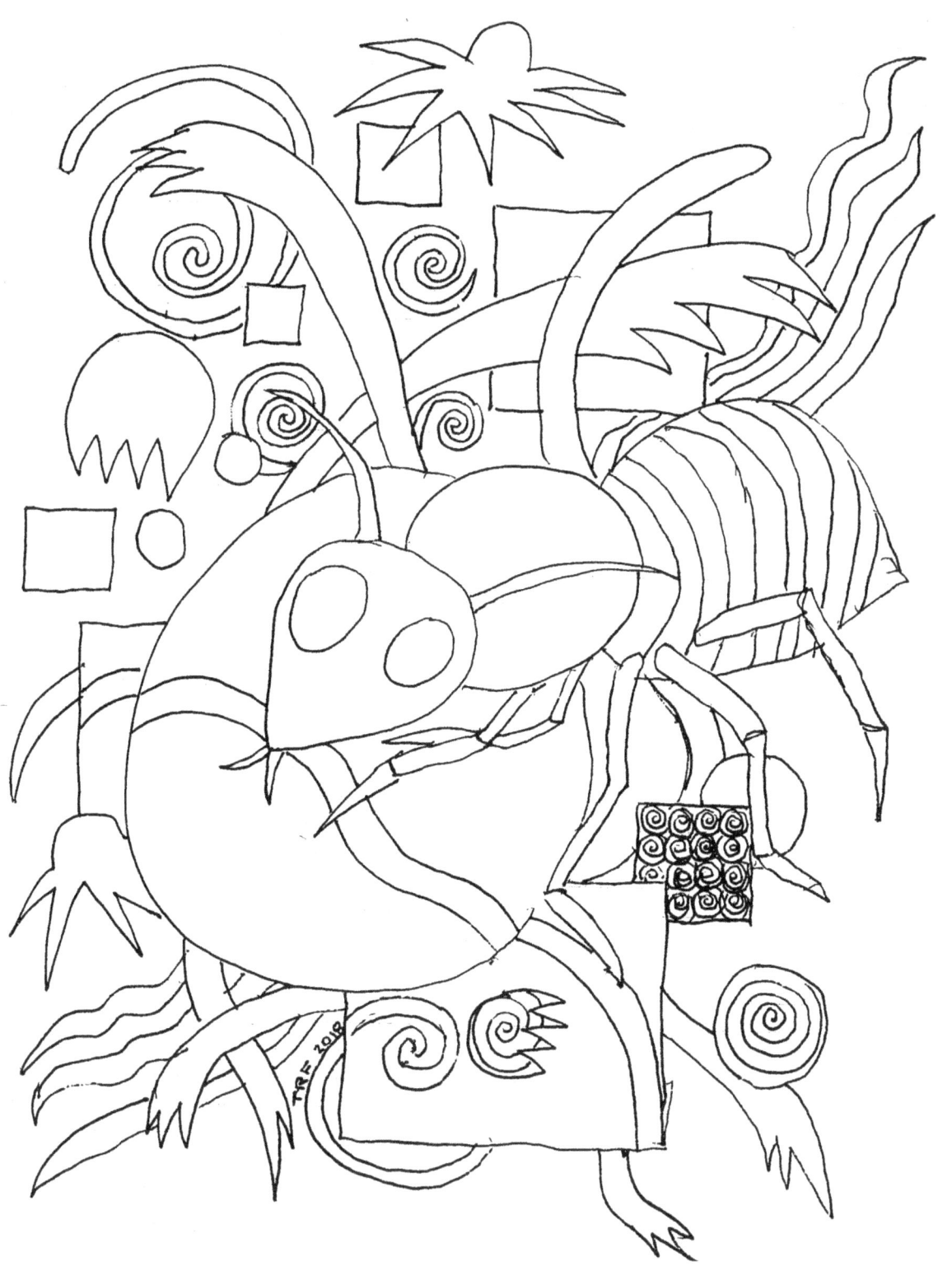

Just don't go
down there.

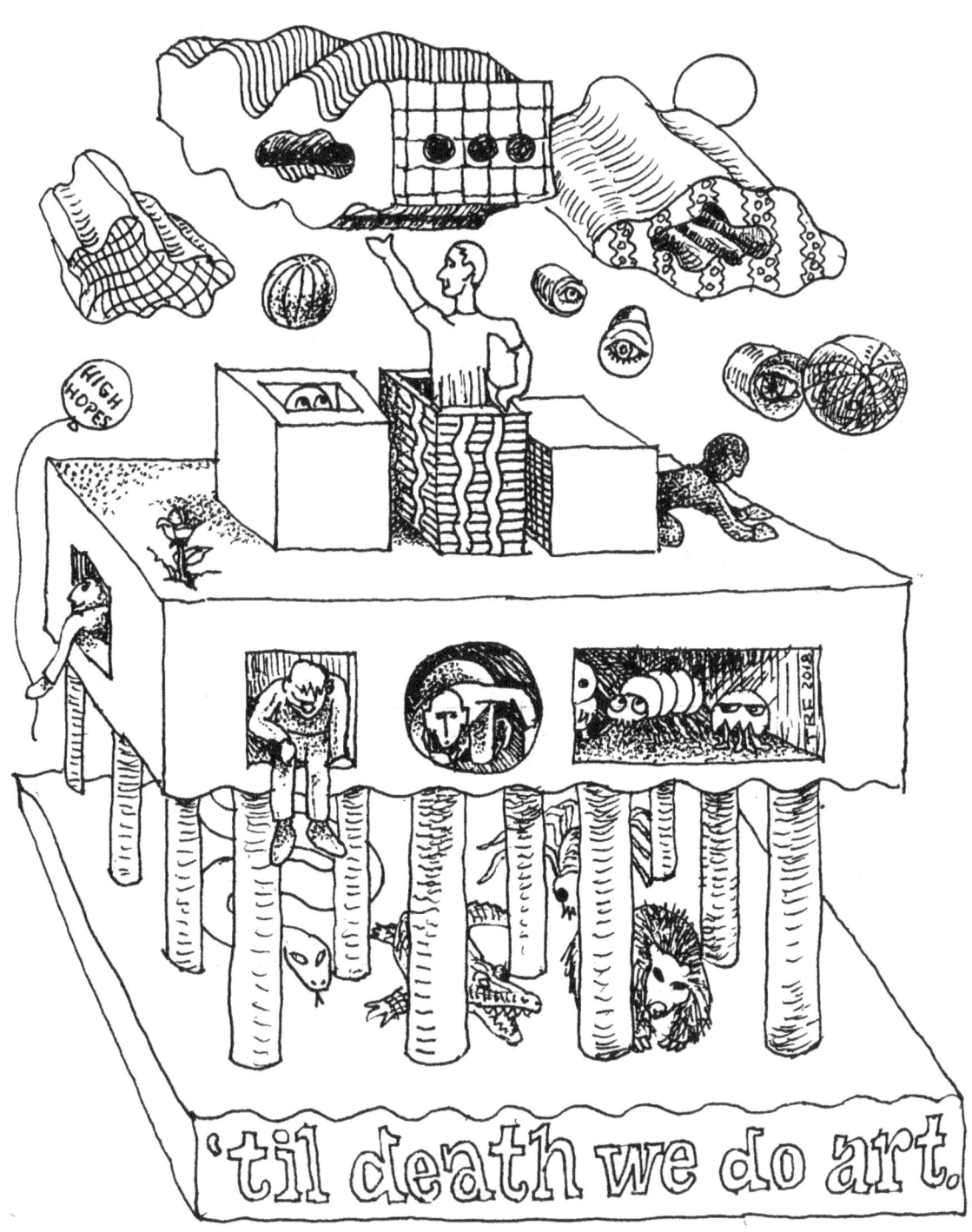

# "Oh, baby, it's a big old goofy world"

JOHN PRINE

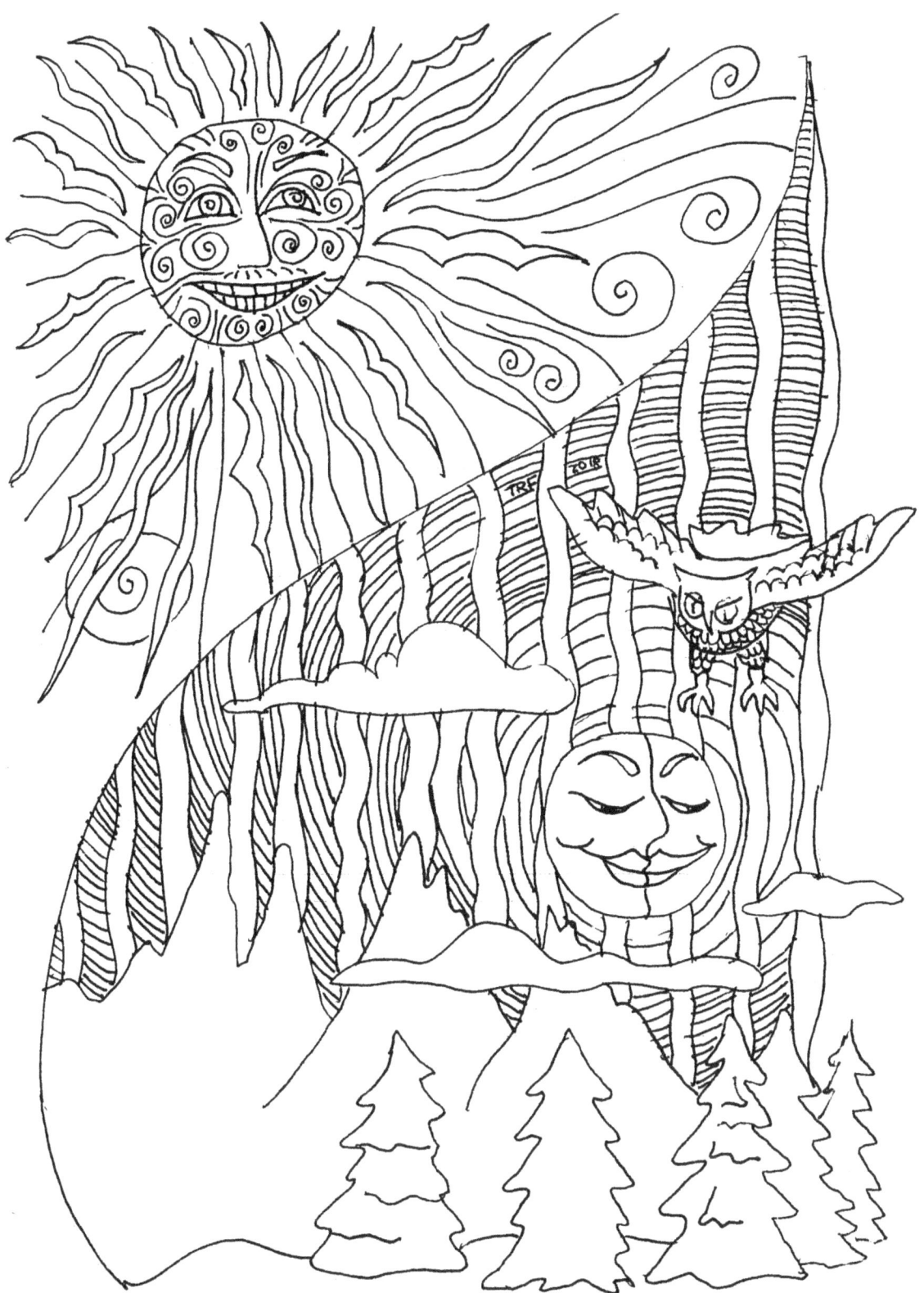

I dare you to work on this
during a very important meeting
while everyone else is taking copious notes.

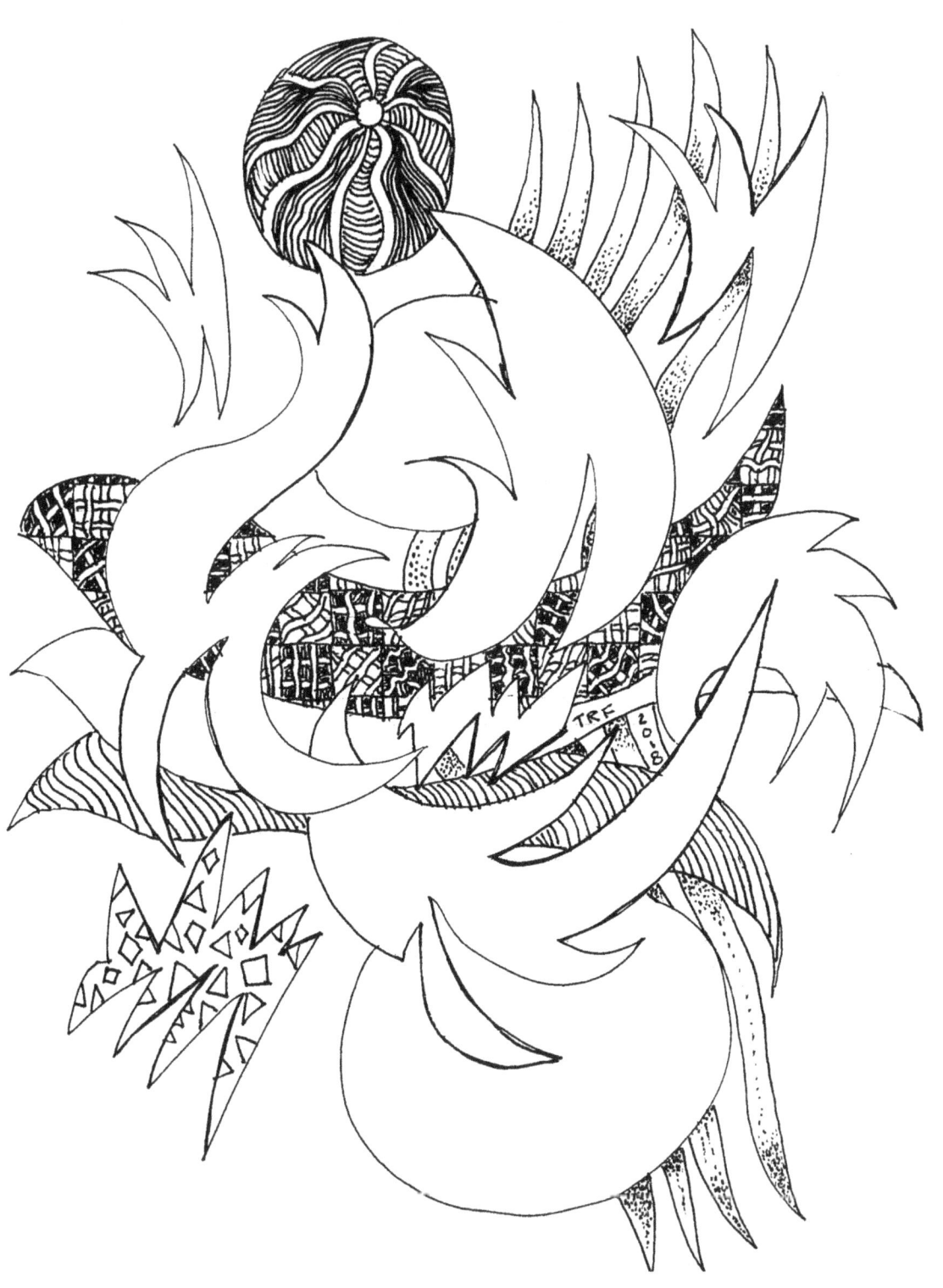

That's all Folks...
Happy trails to you!

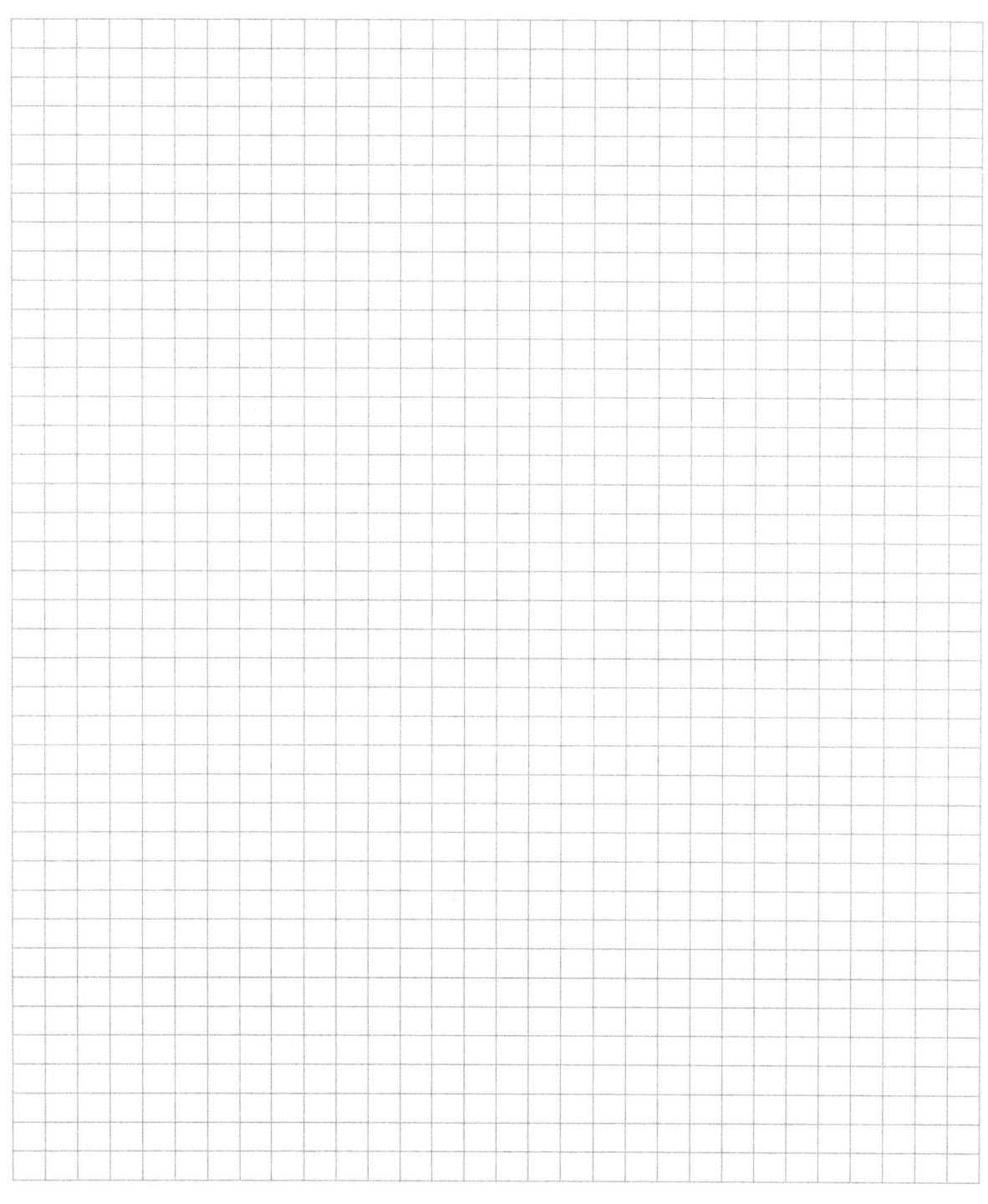

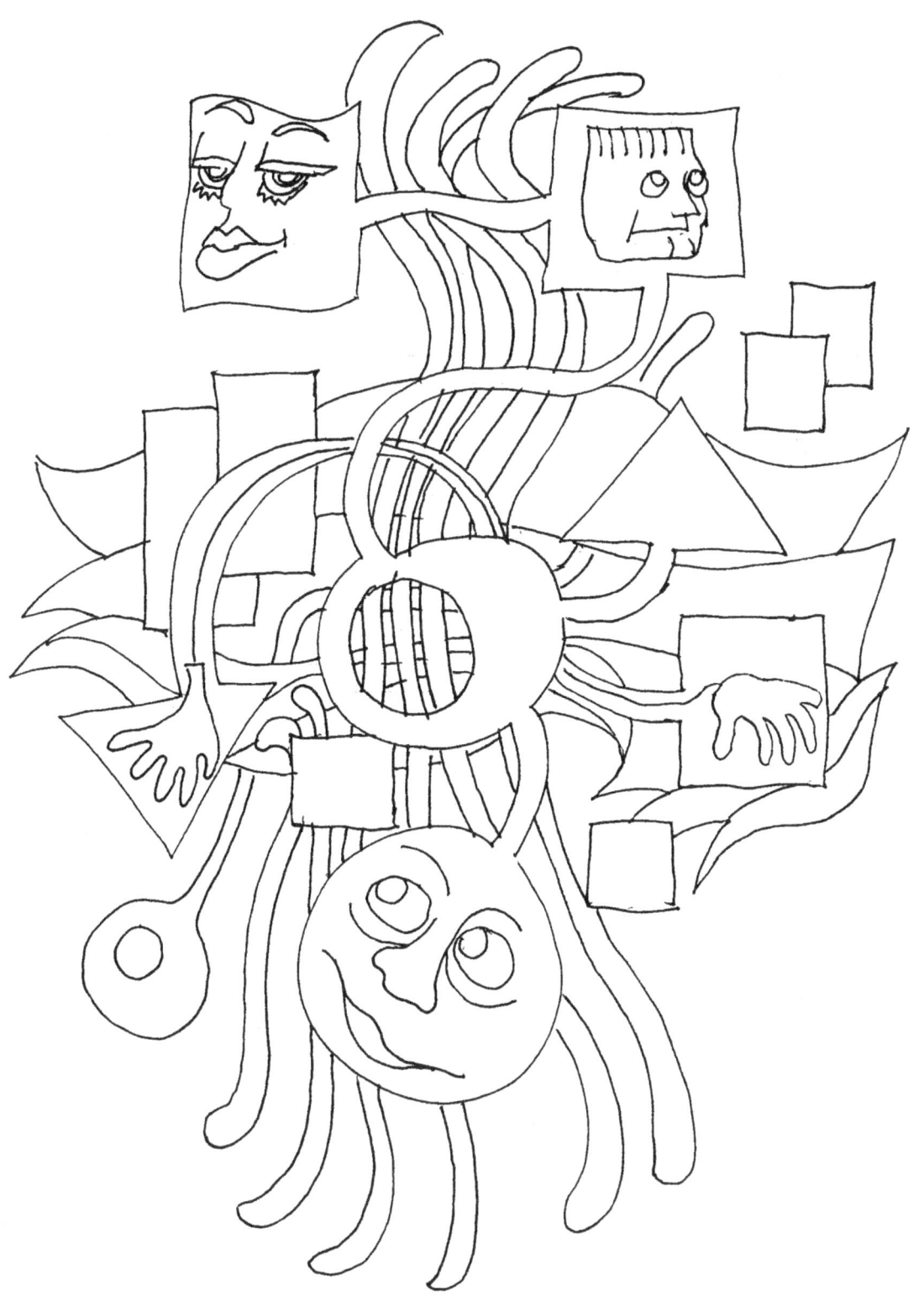

# Congratulations, You Made it this Far!

Hey, Let's stay in touch. If you want to show off your colorized version of these drawings, let me know. Find me on Facebook: @1artguy. or email me: sales@texastproducts.com.

I will keep you posted on Facebook about other projects and products available now and coming soon. Be sure to check out the "til death we do art" garments I created.

I am really honored that I got to collaborate with you to make art.

T.R.F.

www.ingramcontent.com/pod-product-compliance
Lightning Source LLC
Chambersburg PA
CBHW062336220526
45469CB00008B/2737